When The Veil Is Taken Away

Biblical Theology and the Spirit-filled Life

But their minds were made dull, for to this day the same veil remains when the old covenant is read. It has not been removed, because only in Christ is it taken away. Even to this day when Moses is read, a veil covers their hearts. But whenever anyone turns to the Lord, the veil is taken away. Now the Lord is the Spirit, and where the Spirit of the Lord is, there is freedom. And we, who with unveiled faces all reflect the Lord's glory, are being transformed into his likeness with ever-increasing glory, which comes from the Lord, who is the Spirit.

(2 Cor. 3:14-18)

First published in Great Britain in 1994
by Kingdom Faith Ministries, Horsham.

Reprinted in 2004 by Kingdom Faith Resources
Roffey Place, Old Crawley Road, Faygate,
Horsham, West Sussex RH12 4RU.
Tel: 01293 854600. Fax: 01293 854610.
E-mail: resources@kingdomfaith.com.
Web Site: www.kingdomfaith.com.

Copyright © 1994 John McKay

All rights reserved. No part of this publication may be reproduced, stored in a retrieval system, or transmitted, in any form or by any means, electronic, mechanical, photocopying, recording or otherwise, without the permission in writing, of The Way of the Spirit or Kingdom Faith.

The Way of the Spirit is part of Kingdom Faith Church Trust,
Registered Charity No. 278746

Scripture taken from the
HOLY BIBLE, NEW INTERNATIONAL VERSION.
Copyright © 1973, 1978, 1984 by
International Bible Society. Used by
permission of Hodder and Stoughton Limited.

ISBN: 0 9522198 1 6

Text set in Times Roman, printed and bound by Kingdom Faith.

CONTENTS

Preface 5
1. Removing the Veil 7
2. Biblical Literalism, Biblical Criticism and Biblical Experience of the Prophetic Dimension 13
3. Shared Experience of the Power of the Holy Spirit 21
4. Shared Experience of the Life and Ministry of Jesus 31
5. Shared Experience of Jesus as Lord 37
6. Shared Experience of God as Father 45
7. The Bible as Prophetic Literature 51
8. The Drama of Salvation or Creating the End-time Church of the Spirit 61
9. The Charismatic, the Academic Theologian and the Word of God 77
10. That You May Have Life 87
    The Way of the Spirit 93

Preface

It is now twenty years since I was baptised in the Holy Spirit. For the first nine of these I was still lecturing in theology at Hull University and so inevitably was much occupied with trying to fit my new-found experience together with the sort of biblical and theological study we do in our universities. It was no easy task.

I found the two uncomfortable companions, like neighbours who acknowledge each other's existence but prefer to live separate lives, not interfering with one another, as it were on opposite sides of a garden wall. It could not be so with me, for in my life critical theology and committed prophetic/charismatic/pentecostal experience had come together under the same roof and the ensuing tensions proved impossible to live with. The result was initially a lot of very deep rethinking and a total reassessment of what we are doing in teaching the Bible to Spirit-filled believers. This book presents some of the conclusions.

I wrote a first draft of it at the end of these nine years, and after a further eleven spent in active gospel-teaching and preaching I still feel it is worth completing, mainly to help students searching for a prophetic approach to studying the Scriptures, and also because I am convinced there is an urgent need for a fresh approach to Bible teaching that will meet the needs of those experiencing the revival of faith that today is running world-wide, almost all of it Pentecostal in origin and inspiration.

The theological viewpoint of this book has been well tested over the past ten years in preaching and teaching that has borne good fruit. It has also produced *The Way of the Spirit Bible Reading Course* which itself is now producing and encouraging preachers and teachers with a living, revival gospel in several parts of the world.

Over these years much has changed. Today there is far more dialogue between charismatics and biblical scholars than there was in the 1970's. In some ways that is good, but in others quite damaging, for compromise resulting from dialogue has so weakened the Charismatic Movement that the term 'charismatic' now prompts correspondingly weak notions about experience of the Holy Spirit. It is, however, hard to find a suitable alternative. 'Pentecostal' evokes thoughts of denominational streams, 'spiritual' is not specific enough, 'revival' fails to highlight baptism in the Spirit and the spiritual gifts. I personally prefer 'prophetic,' though to some that might imply limiting the Spirit's activity to one particular gift. In this discussion the terms prophetic, charismatic, pentecostal and spiritual are for the most part used interchangeably, except when the specific reference of each is necessitated by the context.

There are basically two ways of studying Scripture. One is objective and analytical, interesting in itself, but imparting little or nothing of the life of God to the student. The other, the way explored here, draws us to God and gives life. When I discovered new life in Christ through the infilling of his Spirit, I knew nothing else would ever satisfy.

John McKay
December 1993

CHAPTER ONE

Removing the Veil

But whenever anyone turns to the Lord, the veil is taken away. Now the Lord is the Spirit . . .

(2 Cor. 3:16f)

About the time renewed faith was leading me out of academic theology to go and preach the gospel, the converse was happening with another Anglican priest/academic who said he had lost his faith. He felt it necessary to relinquish his holy orders, but did not feel any corresponding necessity to cease teaching theology in university. That is quite simply because academic theology can be taught and studied without faith. It is, after all, a purely mental discipline, in theory at any rate.

Conflict of Theology and Faith

In a university theology department students are taught to analyse the text of Scripture as objectively and critically as possible. Efforts to stimulate faith are usually discouraged on the grounds that anyone, Christian, Muslim, Buddhist, atheist, agnostic, or whatever, should be as free to study theology as he is to study history or philosophy or any other degree subject. In practice most students do have some kind of Christian faith, though by no means all, while the number of lecturers who would admit to active Christian commitment is also not negligible. However, the qualifications required for studying theology are not belief or religious devotion, but so many A-levels, as is only right and proper in an academic institution. The debate whether this state of affairs is also right from a Christian viewpoint is an old one and I do not wish to get involved in it here. My concern is simply to discuss the problems it raises for Spirit-filled Christians.

In contrast with my ex-priest colleague, I found it increasingly difficult to be purely academic about my faith, because the Spirit was speaking to me about loving, setting captives free, opening blind eyes and glorifying Jesus, which are hardly the sort of exercises one usually associates with university departments. It is often said that charismatics are strong on praise, but weak on theology. I would rather say they are strong on praise and strong on their own brand of theology, but unhappy about the sort of dispassionate, uncommitted theology one frequently encounters in an academic setting. In theory a pentecostal theologian should have no problem about teaching in a seminary, but in practice much of the theology taught in ministerial training centres differs little in approach from that found in universities. There is clearly a tension that needs to be resolved. It is with such matters that this book is concerned.

Dialogue without Compromise—the Analogy of Drama

It seems to me that the two things, academic biblical study (whether pursued by liberal or conservative scholars makes little difference) and prophetic Christianity, operate at two very different levels. I see a kind of analogy with the world of drama, the academic being in some ways like the reviewer whose task is to analyse, criticise and comment on the play, the charismatic more like the producer or the performer on stage. One individual may attempt to handle each of these functions separately at different times, but he will have great difficulty in doing them both together. Inevitably there must be a great deal of tension between the two, though it is hoped that in the end they might function to each other's mutual benefit, even if at times criticism and hurt may be the more apparent marks of their relationship.

Since my training is in biblical theology, I limit myself exclusively to that. Whether my views apply equally to wider areas of theological study, I must leave others more competent than myself to judge.

Now in this context of biblical theology I should be quite unhappy with any theological position that is based on compromise or ideals about a middle way. Indeed I should regard such a theology as being as worthless as the opinion of a middle-man between an actor and a drama-critic, for he would be neither one nor the other and equally useless to both. However, if compromise is unacceptable, there is the obvious danger that the academic's arguments might so undermine the faith of the charismatic that he cease to function as one, or conversely that the charismatic might so dogmatically oppose the academic's opinions that he become unwilling even to countenance rational, theological assessment. We see both tendencies operating from time to time among theological students in particular, but also among Christians in general. In the field of drama responses like these would either cause the play's performance to deteriorate from lack of attention to criticism, or to collapse altogether through defection of the actors.

Somehow charismatics and academic theologians must learn to live together, even if in a state of tension, like actors and their critics. That may prove not too difficult so long as the academic and the charismatic are two separate people, but the problem takes on a totally different look when they become one and the same person. That was my own problem, but it is one that is becoming more widespread as the influence of prophetic Christianity grows. So in a sense this is an autobiographical work, since it is written from personal experience as well as from academic reflection. As such it should be of some value to others who are either charismatics or academics, even if they are not both, especially since they do tend to brush shoulders with each other increasingly in our time.

Biblical Scholarship and Revelation from the Spirit

This study divides into two main sections. The first (chs. 2-6) is concerned with the task of outlining the viewpoint from which a charismatic approaches his Bible. I have defined that in terms of 'shared experience' and have attempted to show how it affects his understanding of his relationship with the Father, the Son and the Holy Spirit as they are met in the pages of Scripture. The second part (chs. 7-9) tries to demonstrate how a charismatic might view the Bible as literature, how he might interpret its central theological theme, and how his viewpoint relates to that of contemporary scholarship.

In reading the views expressed in these chapters, it should be borne in mind that they are not all based on the findings of academic scholarship. Many of them are based on realisations that have resulted from my own experience of the Holy Spirit. 'Revelation' is the only word I know that adequately expresses their source, even if that may sound pretentious to some people; but at the same time it would be quite untruthful for me to deny a considerable amount of intellectual reflection as well. A much better way of explaining what I mean is to use an expression of Paul's, the one that furnishes the title of this book, concerning the removal of a veil. In 2 Cor. 3:14-18 he contrasts the understanding with which the Bible (the Old Testament only in his day) is read before and after 'anyone turns to the Lord'. He says that beforehand it is read as it were with a veil over the mind, but afterwards with the veil removed. He attributes the change to the action of the Spirit, for, he says, 'the Lord is the Spirit', and he goes on to speak about contemplating the Lord's glory, presumably in the reading of Scripture, since that is what the paragraph is all about.[1] Then emphatically he reiterates that this 'comes from the Lord, who is the Spirit'. The message is clear enough, that the Spirit enables us to read the Bible with some new clarity that could not be possible without his aid.

Now charismatics commonly do speak of some disclosure experience similar to Paul's when they read the Bible after baptism in the Spirit. They tell of passages illuminated in new ways, of texts that take on new meaningfulness, of verses that burn themselves into the memory, of completely new appreciations of whole books of the Bible, of a positive urge to read page after page of the text, of exciting new discoveries about God's self-revelation in Scripture, and so forth. The charismatic

---

[1] NIV translates 'reflect the Lord's glory'. NIV footnote suggests 'contemplate', cp. RSV 'beholding'.

who speaks enthusiastically of his latest insights from reading Habakkuk or Jude will tell how before baptism in the Spirit some months earlier he did not even know these books existed, or certainly that he had no idea about what was in them, let alone that they held such spiritual treasures.

For my own part, I well recall, for example, having spent three years as a Ph.D. student mulling over Deuteronomy (among other things), and then on re-reading it some years later in the light of my experience of the Holy Spirit, being surprised to discover the immense spiritual treasures in it that I had simply failed to appreciate before. Indeed I can honestly say that I came to understand more, not just about the content of Deuteronomy, but about the content of almost every other book in the Bible, and particularly in the New Testament, in the months following my own experience of Pentecost, than I had in all my years of theological study. There was certainly some kind of veil removed, for it was one of the most exciting and memorable experiences of my life rereading the Bible from cover to cover, genealogies, statistics, priestly regulations and all, and finding in it, chapter after chapter, treasures I never realised existed. Furthermore, where before there had been only dim perception of the Bible's meaning as a whole, or no perception at all, now it all seemed to make excellent sense. The rest of this book represents an attempt to give a rough outline of the sort of sense I now find it makes.[2]

---

[2] For fuller discussion, see John McKay, *The Way of the Spirit* (four volumes), Kingdom Faith, 1988-1990, which covers each biblical book, tracing its charismatic dynamic in much fuller detail.

CHAPTER TWO

Biblical Literalism, Biblical Criticism

and

Biblical Experience of the Prophetic Dimension

We have not received the spirit of the world but the Spirit who is from God, that we may understand what God has freely given us. This is what we speak, not in words taught by human wisdom but in words taught by the Spirit, expressing spiritual truths to spiritual men.[3]

(1 Cor. 2:12-13)

It is often said that charismatics have no adequate doctrine of Scripture, which is in some ways true, though perhaps it would be more accurate to say they have problems with all existing doctrines of Scripture. That is not always because they consider them wrong, but rather because they find them insufficient for explaining their own appreciation of God's word. Since charismatics are drawn from a wide variety of backgrounds, some of them are fundamentalists, others are rationalists or liberals, and others are of every shade of opinion in between. Most, however, would express some frustration about the inadequacy of the traditional modes of interpretation they have inherited for describing their own views. Now this problem arises mainly because prophetic understanding operates on a different plane from all others.

The Academic Approach

The fundamentalist maintains a doctrine of literal inspiration of Scripture in all its detail, whether theological, historical or scientific, and so, for example, would argue that the world was created literally in six

---

[3] So NIV footnote, cp. RSV. NIV text reads 'in spiritual words'.

days, that there was actually a primogenital pair named Adam and Eve who originally lived in a garden called Eden which must at one time have been geographically locatable, that men really did begin to speak different languages when a tower at Babel fell down, and so forth. To the fundamentalist the laws of Israel were dictated word for word by God to Moses on Mount Sinai, and in a similar fashion the utterances of the prophets are the very speeches of God himself. Thus every word of Scripture is cherished as an infallible word of God to be read, studied, learned and obeyed, but not criticised or questioned.

By contrast the rationalist maintains that everything in the Bible should be open to criticism. He holds that it contains the depositions of men who were poets, philosophers, theologians, historians and the like, and that their writings should be read and analysed in much the same way as those of any other poets, philosophers, theologians and historians. Thus the Bible is seen as a record of the reflections of religious men about God, rather than of the revelations of God himself to men, and it is sacred not because it is God-given, but because it has become hallowed by centuries of tradition and use. According to this view the laws of Israel were simply accumulated over the generations, but, because of the sanctity of the memory of Moses, became attached to his name. Similarly, the utterances of the prophets are the collected poems and sayings of literary men, well trained in the art of poetry, and to a lesser extent of prose-writing, men who also had some shrewd insight into matters political and theological. Thus, for example, Amos was probably no simple shepherd receiving messages from heaven, but a man of some culture and learning, perhaps a leisured sheep-farm owner, who had the time and freedom to devote to theological speculation. His writings should therefore be read with the same open critical eye with which one might read the works of any modern-day Bonhoeffer or Barth.

Between these extremes of interpretation lies a whole array of intermediate opinions that tend to one side or the other. Views that lean towards fundamentalism are usually called 'conservative', while the rationalist tendency is known as 'liberal'. The conservative tendency is

Biblical Literalism, Criticism and Experience

sometimes also referred to as 'literalist' and the liberal as 'critical', or even 'radical'. Conservative opinion tends to be strongest in the evangelical wing of the churches, liberal in the non-evangelical. Set side by side these varied views form a complete spectrum of biblical interpretation. It may therefore seem surprising that the charismatic, or indeed any one at all, should find nowhere in its modulating shades of opinion where he feels entirely happy and at home.

This spectrum is, however, a fairly modern one. While it is possible to detect precursors to it in the writings of particular theologians down the centuries, particularly since the Reformation, it is only one that has held centre stage in the past 150 years. Liberal theology only began to become influential in the second half of the last century and fundamentalism was born as a reaction to it at the beginning of this. In earlier times the liberal/conservative debate would have attracted little attention.

There is an older form of interpretation, popular before the Reformation and still sometimes used today, that sits loose to such questions about literal, historical value, neither affirming nor denying the Bible's accuracy at these levels. This kind of interpretation is almost entirely occupied with tracing hidden, spiritual meanings in the text. For example, it would see the real value of the flood story, not in that it preserves a record of something that happened long ago, but in that it symbolises or foreshadows the saving work of the Church. In this view the ark carrying Noah and his family through the flood-waters to safety becomes a prototype of the Church carrying Christians through the water of baptism to salvation. In a similar way the restored Jerusalem of the Old Testament prophets' visions becomes a portrayal of the heavenly Jerusalem of Christian end-time hope. Among the more common terms used to denote such spiritualising interpretation are 'typology', 'allegory' and 'anagogy'. Limited examples of these methods are found in the New Testament itself, for instance, in Paul's figurative use of the stories about Sarah and Hagar in Gal. 3:21-31, or Peter's use of the flood story in 1 Pet. 3:20f, or Hebrews' use of the laws of temple, priesthood and sacrifice in chs. 7-10. However, this form of interpretation is rarely used today, except occasionally in preaching, and to the modern mind it seems esoteric and antiquated.

The charismatic would also find such older methods a bit awkward, for he is as much the contemporary Christian as any. He may indeed be spiritually very sensitive, but he is also a historical realist and would tend to start from the literal sense of the text in much the same way as the present-day conservative or liberal. It is not because of any desire to retreat into spiritualising that he feels uncomfortable in the company of modern biblical interpreters. What then is his problem?

The Prophetic Mentality

The answer to that question is quite simply that he is a prophet, or is at least prophetically sympathetic, and so reads his Bible with the eye and intellect of a prophetical person. Let me illustrate what that means. Once in a conversation about a lecture course on mysticism a colleague remarked to me in some frustration, 'How can our students ever hope to understand mysticism? Surely only mystics themselves can properly appreciate the records of mystical visionaries. It must take a mystic to understand the mystics!' The charismatic might expostulate similarly about the Bible (or much of it), that only prophetical persons can properly appreciate the records of prophetical men. Or again, another academic, a New Testament scholar with pentecostal sympathies, once spoke to me of his exasperation when reading the works of fellow New Testament scholars who have no clear appreciation of the prophetic mentality of people like Luke or Paul or John.

Of course, to the non-charismatic such an attitude will seem exclusivist and arrogant, but it is very much in tune with similar viewpoints expressed by prophetical men in other times. For example, Tertullian in the early third century spoke of a division between the spiritual Christians of his own (Montanist) church and the 'natural' believers (*psychici*) in the other churches and claimed that only the former truly

Biblical Literalism, Criticism and Experience

appreciated what the Spirit of God was saying to the faithful.[4] Similar sentiments are also found in the writings of Ireneus in the late second[5], but even before that we find something much the same in the New Testament itself. Paul appears to have been the one who first introduced the distinction when he wrote to the Corinthian church: 'The man without the Spirit (*psychikos*) does not accept the things that come from the Spirit of God, for they are foolishness to him, and he cannot understand them, because they are spiritually discerned. The spiritual man (*pneumatikos*) makes judgements about all things' (or perhaps better 'has the measure of them all'; 1 Cor. 2:14f). Jude also draws a distinction between those who 'follow mere natural instincts' and those who 'have the Spirit' (Jude 19).

This is the context in which the charismatic's dilemma must be understood. To him the bulk of current biblical interpretation, whether conservative or liberal, is the work of the natural mind searching for meaning in God's word using the common techniques of scholarship shared with other secular disciplines, such as history, literary criticism, or philosophy. This kind of investigation has immense value and it

---

[4] Cp. Tertullian, *Against Praxeas* 1: 'As for me, I was thereafter separated from the *psychici* because of my acknowledgement and my defence of the Paraclete.' Tertullian, *Against Marcion* IV.22: 'For when a man is rapt in the Spirit, especially when he beholds the glory of God, or when God speaks through him, he inevitably loses the customary operation of his senses—is bound to, indeed, because he is overshadowed with the power of God. There is some dispute between ourselves and the *psychici* about this.'

[5] Ireneus, *Against Heresies* V.6.1, (cited in Eusebius, *Ecclesiastical History* V.7.2): 'The Apostle says, "We speak wisdom among the perfect." [1 Cor. 2:6] The ones he calls "perfect" are those who have received the Spirit of God and who through the Spirit of God speak in all languages, just as he also used to do himself. In the same way we also hear many brethren in the Church who possess prophetic gifts, and speak through the Spirit in all kinds of languages, and bring to light the secret things of men for their good, and declare the mysteries of God. The Apostle also calls these men "spiritual"—they are spiritual because they partake of the Spirit.'

would be totally misguided to underrate it, but the charismatic finds himself frustrated in the face of it, since it by-passes and fails to recognise a complete dimension that he himself sees so very clearly in his Bible, indeed the one he regards as the most important of all, in the light of which he would wish all else to be viewed, the dimension he might call the spiritual (*pneumatikon*), or the charismatic, or the prophetic.

As I try to give this dimension more concrete conceptual definition, I feel, very much like Paul, that that would be more effectively done 'not in words taught us by human wisdom but in words taught by the Spirit' (1 Cor. 2:13). In its light I sometimes find the conservative's views easier to sustain, occasionally the liberal's, but more frequently neither. It would be wrong to think of it only as a yardstick for measuring opinions of liberals and conservatives against each other, for it operates at a different level altogether and often has just nothing to say about the arguments of scholarship at all. Conservatism is a theology of biblical literalism, liberalism a theology of biblical criticism, but I would call the charismatic's approach a theology of biblical experience—or perhaps better 'shared experience'. That aptly expresses his awareness of the similarity between his own experience and that of the prophets, apostles and Jesus, and also his awareness of being himself an active participant in the same drama in which they were involved, of playing the same sort of part as they played in it, and of doing so in the same prophetic manner. All will become clearer as we proceed.

Besides the self-consciously liberal, conservative and pentecostal approaches to the Bible, there is also a popular view held by the vast majority of Western Christians today. It is not clearly thought out, mainly because churchmen have not been encouraged to get involved in theological debate about the Bible. In consequence they tend to hold opinions that are broadly conservative, though generally based on sketchy knowledge of the Scriptures and held with much puzzlement and with many reservations about the value of what they read. To them conservatives believe too much, liberals too little, and pentecostals with too great enthusiasm. My debate is not with them, for their views are not particularly articulate. However, they too are fellow travellers on the Christian journey and, along with liberals and conservatives, have their part to play in the unfolding drama of salvation. I intend no implication that pentecostals alone have that privilege. However, I do believe they have a distinctive view of the Bible and a peculiar role in the Church, and here we are primarily concerned with defining that view and that role and with determining how they relate to the views and roles others play, especially those of conservative and liberal theologians, whose voices are the ones most loudly heard in Bible teaching today.

CHAPTER THREE

Shared Experience of the Power of the Holy Spirit

And you will receive the gift of the Holy Spirit. The promise is for you and your children and for all who are far off—for all whom the Lord our God will call.

(Acts 2:38f)

On the day of Pentecost Peter invited his hearers with these words to share in the apostles' experience of the Holy Spirit. Pentecostals claim that the invitation is still open and that acceptance of it radically changes a Christian's view, not only of his own faith, but also of the faith of the early New Testament Church, and even of the prophetic personalities of the Old Testament.

Charismatic Appreciation of the Gifts of the Spirit.

At the simplest level, the one at which most people first encounter them, charismatics have a particular understanding of the gifts of the Spirit. To many Christians the lists of spiritual gifts in passages like Rom. 12:6-8 or 1 Cor. 12:7-11 are largely enigmatic. To some they savour of primitive religious behaviour which was outgrown as the Church developed in maturity. To others they read like a catalogue of wondrous experiences one usually associates with some mythical golden age of the past but which bears no vital relation to modern reality. To others they are simply a long forgotten mystery, as indeed they were already to Chrysostom at the end of the fourth century. Commenting on 1 Cor. 12:1ff, he wrote, 'This whole passage is exceedingly obscure; and the obscurity is occasioned by our ignorance of such things which, though they were common in those days, are no longer happening in our own.'[6]

---

[6] Chrysostom, *Commentary on 1 Corinthians.*

However, most Christians today would not be able to express their opinions about the gifts with any clarity at all and would hold some confused blend of all these opinions.

There are many, on the other hand, who do have very carefully thought out doctrines explaining the disappearance of the gifts from the early Church. They maintain the gifts were given to encourage Christians in the apostolic age until what Paul calls 'perfection' should come (1 Cor. 13:10), and for the sake of their argument evangelicals identify that as the completed New Testament, while catholics identify it with Mother Church and its episcopal system. Once these were established, they argue, the gifts were no longer needed and so were withdrawn by God himself. Some go even further and state that any modern-day manifestation of the gifts must therefore be counterfeit, not of God, and even of the devil. Apart from this misuse of one verse, there is, of course, no biblical support whatsoever for such teaching, and the rest of this book will show that indeed the contrary is the biblical truth.

My own attitude in the 1960's was probably of the 'confused blend', but in the early 1970's I came into contact with an ever increasing number of Christians who claimed a spiritual endowment that gave them access to similar gifts today. Then I experienced some of these gifts myself and I vividly remember being quite startled by my discovery of what they really were. That, however, is another tale for another time. The important point here is perhaps best summarised in a Job-like confession that to that point I had heard of these things with my ears, but now I could say, 'My eyes have seen.' (cp. Job 42:5) That is to say, before that time I had a theological or intellectual attitude to such matters, however confused or dimly perceived, but now they had become a living part of my own experience. Or, to put it another way, I had accepted Peter's invitation and was beginning to learn something of the extent of its implications.

Quite apart from being surprised to discover just how different the spiritual gifts looked from the inside than they had formerly appeared from the outside, I was now for the first time, in a fairly elementary way, made aware of the challenge that shared experience presented to traditional biblical interpretation. To begin with, I could no longer acquiesce in the views about the gifts held by non-charismatics and found myself instantly dissatisfied with almost every commentary on the subject that I read. Since I now knew for myself that the gifts were a living part of Christian experience available today as well as in the first century, I could no longer even discuss the possibility that they might be simply an expression of primitive religion or of a lost idyllic age of the Church's early history, and certainly not that they were unintelligible. Of course, the mere experience of such phenomena as tongues, prophecy, supernormal knowledge and healing was in itself no guarantee that these were the same gifts as those known to the earliest Christians, but at least the possibility was now worth exploring, and the further I looked, the more convinced I became that I was indeed sharing experiences of the same genre as those, not only of the early Christians, but also of the Old Testament prophets and of Jesus himself.

Charismatic Understanding of Baptism in the Spirit.

For convenience, the activity of the Holy Spirit is usually divided into three broad aspects catalogued under the headings 'baptism in the Spirit', 'gifts of the Spirit' and 'fruit of the Spirit'. The first of these relates to an experience of spiritual illumination and enduement similar to that of the apostles on the day of Pentecost in Acts 2, of the Samaritan converts in Acts 8, of Cornelius and his household in Acts 10, or of the Ephesian disciples in Acts 19. In these and other passages it is described in terms of being filled with the Holy Spirit, or of being endued with power from on high, manifesting itself in supernatural expression through utterances in strange languages or through prophecy, of being inspired with boldness to proclaim God's word, and to call on the sick to rise healed, and above all of a special awareness of God's presence in a measure hitherto unknown. A typical charismatic testimony might tell of an overwhelming sense of God's nearness, of being loved, of happiness welling up inside, of a sense of strong confidence in God, of a knowledge of release from fear and guilt, of an outflow of joyous praise, perhaps of an urge to prophesy or speak in tongues or to sing or to tell someone else, but above all of a confirmation of belief in God and Christ that virtually turns belief into knowledge. And so the charismatic feels that he shares the experience of the disciples at Pentecost who were so happy that they were thought to be drunk, or of Cornelius and his family who erupted into tongues and prophesied, or of the apostle John who was caught up in the Spirit on the Lord's day, or even of some Old Testament personalities like Ezekiel who saw visions of God in his glory, or of Moses who heard the voice of God himself.

Some charismatics speak of a once for all baptism in the Spirit, others tell of repeated baptisms, but all of them bear witness that they know what the prophet Joel meant when he said the outpouring of the Spirit would be accompanied by dreams, visions and prophecies (Joel 2:28). The miraculous and the supernatural in Scripture readily become part of the charismatic's shared experience. He dreams significant dreams that are more than mere phantoms of the night, but tell of God and his will, he sees mystic visions of the Lord in his holiness and he hears the voice of God speaking sometimes audibly, but more normally in the silence of his heart. I refuse to recognise mere psychological explanations for these experiences, because, like the similar phenomena of which Paul speaks in 1 Cor. 14, they edify and build up the believer and the community of believers in their faith in God and their love for one another.

Of course there can be a quite human element in all this, even a spurious one. That has led many to dismiss prophetic Christianity as counterfeit, but the same problem was present in ancient times and the Bible's answer to it is certainly not to reject the Spirit's work. On the contrary it bids us sift and discern what is of God and hold on to that: 'Do not put out the Spirit's fire; do not treat prophecies with contempt. Test everything. Hold on to the good.' (1 Thes. 5:19-21) John tells us to test the spirits whether they glorify the incarnate and risen Christ (1 John 4:1-3), and when that is done it becomes immediately clear just how much present-day charismatic activity is indeed very genuine. The same may be said about tongues, which can be similarly tested with the Pauline thermometer: How much does it edify the speaker in his relationship with his Lord? (1 Cor. 14:1-5)

Shared experience extends beyond private, mystical and revelatory events. Miraculous mediation of the word and power of God to others, through prophecy, healings and the like, becomes an every-day part of the charismatic's ministry. We do not often hear of walking on water, but we do encounter healings, some of them very spectacular, occasionally the raising of the dead, also miraculous communication across language barriers, stories of supernatural protection in times of danger, gifts of supernormal knowledge and perception, especially of a sort that bring unbelievers to conviction or that lead to healing and so forth.

Charismatic Experience of the Fruit of the Spirit.

If the charismatic's experience of baptism in the Spirit and the gifts of the Spirit have a clear New Testament ring, so also does his experience of what Paul calls 'the fruit of the Spirit' (Gal. 5:22). The apostle speaks of the Spirit cultivating in the believer such characteristics as love, joy, peace, patience, kindness, goodness, faithfulness, gentleness and self-control. Similarly, in John's Gospel we find teaching about a peace that surpasses anything the world has to offer (John 14:27) and about a joy that is complete (15:11), a joy no man can take away (16:22). It is significant that Jesus speaks of these things in the context of his discourse about the Spirit (chs. 14-16), for it is invariably part of a charismatic's testimony that such teaching as Paul or John gives on these matters gains new, personal meaningfulness after baptism in the Spirit, often in ways the new-born charismatic had not hitherto realised possible. For example, he will probably tell of a new joy in worship, whether public or private, even an exuberance that rises in praise to God, like the streams of living water that Jesus mentions elsewhere (7:37-9). He will also tell of a new sense of tranquillity he has gained from his new vivid awareness of the proximity of God. But above all he will claim a new appreciation of the reality of divine love, a love that is particularly operative among the brethren (1 John 3:11ff), but which also spills over to all men. Charismatic groups and churches are well-known for the strength of their fellowship and the warmth of love that exists in them, all of which they claim derives from their awareness of being a body knit together by the Spirit of Christ.

Charismatic Views of Biblical Experience.

Now that all sounds exceedingly dramatic, as indeed it is, but the effects of such shared experience for biblical interpretation are also dramatic, though in a very different way. It becomes increasingly difficult for instance, for a liberal theologian who experiences this dimension to view the miraculous and supernatural elements in the Old and New Testaments in terms of mythology or legend, for example, and one immediate temptation is for him to jettison all his scholarship and become a fundamentalist. Some do fall to this temptation, though the step is not a necessary one. Fundamentalists make doctrinal claims, charismatics experiential. No charismatic could ever appeal to his shared experience to uphold such doctrines or prove such facts as the fundamentalist cherishes, for example the scientific veracity of the creation narrative in Gen. 1, or the literal existence of a fish that could carry Jonah in its belly without harming him. Prophetic insight has very little to say about such matters, though it does warm instantly to the emphasis on God's goodness in the creation story or to the message in the Book of Jonah about the need for obedience in a prophet. Prophetic experience does not destroy or by-pass man's reasoning faculty! It is still possible for charismatics to remain fairly liberal in their theological views, as some actually do.

None the less, the major effect of shared experience is to make the charismatic treasure parts of the biblical record he might beforehand have viewed with much scepticism. Not only the miracle stories in the gospels, but those actions attributed to the power of the Spirit in Acts and the prophetic narratives in the Old Testament also become particularly precious. Tales of visions or encounters with God, such as we find in the stories of Abraham's conversations with God, Jacob's ladder, Moses at the burning bush, the boy Samuel in the temple, Elisha and the chariots of fire, Isaiah's vision of the LORD on his throne, Habakkuk's warrior-God, Zechariah's night visions, Daniel's angelic visitations, the transfigured Christ, Peter at Joppa, Paul at Troas—such and other similar stories take on a new feel of authenticity, because so many charismatics have their own tales which, though not identical, are of the same genre.

As we have seen, something similar might be said of stories about healings and other miraculous happenings, such as we find in the Elijah and Elisha stories in 1 Kings 17 to 2 Kings 9, or in the Acts of the Apostles, many of which are commonly dismissed in academic circles as of questionable historical value. In a similar way, the charismatic will tell that he has some kind of empathetic appreciation of what happened to the seventy elders at the tent of meeting in Num. 11, or that he can understand the behaviour of the prophets whom Saul met coming down from the sanctuary at Gibeah prophesying to the accompaniment of their lyres, tambourines, flutes and harps in 1 Sam. 10. He will insist that their conduct was not at all 'frenzied' and that it had nothing to do with primitive, ecstatic, religious practices, as is often said, but that it was charismatic in much the same sense as the conduct of the disciples at Pentecost was, or as is the conduct of happy worshippers at a charismatic church service today.

One area where shared experience completely transforms biblical interpretation is that of the prophetic word. As has already been noted, the liberal views prophecy as something inspirational only in a very loose and vague sense, relating it more to natural sagacity, shrewd insight and inherited traditions, than to anything else. Prophetic experience, however, encourages a very different view, for the mediation of messages directly received is of the very essence of charismatic prophecy. Sometimes these messages are delivered in verse form, sometimes in prose, sometimes only the gist of the message is given and not in any particularly marked style, but always there is something received, some direct revelation that is passed on. Sometimes it will be communicated immediately, at others it will be kept for a later occasion when the brethren are assembled together to hear it. Charismatic prophecy is something like the rehearsing of a conversation with a friend, only in this instance the friend is the Lord himself. 'Thus says the Lord' means literally that to the charismatic, and so to him the liberal view of prophecy must remain entirely inadequate.

Equally, however, the charismatic would find it hard to acquiesce in the fundamentalist view of literal, mechanical inspiration, as though God had precisely dictated every single word that is spoken. On some rare occasions it may seem like that, but generally the dictum of Paul holds good, that 'the spirits of prophets are subject to the control of prophets' (1 Cor. 14:32). The charismatic will tell that he speaks his prophecy in faith, that is that it is indeed a word from God. Pressed about his utterance he would normally admit that, while he believes it comes from God, it is not always possible to draw an absolute line of demarcation between what in it is from God and what from himself. The utterance is certainly inspired, but it is filtered through a human channel, with the result that it is in the end only a near, hopefully very near, approximation to what God wants to communicate. Or as Paul puts it in 1 Cor. 13:9, 'we prophesy in part' (i.e. imperfectly). That helps us understand why George gives his prophecy in King James' English, Mary hers in her local dialect, William his in cultured speech; or why Isaiah spoke with a Hebrew style quite different from Ezekiel's. The prophet's rehearsal of what God has said to him will have a degree of precision similar to the degree of exactitude he might attain in reporting some important conversation, a degree that will vary from person to person, and will even vary according to the mood of the speaker.

Now at this point we are confronted with the problem of determining how much any prophecy is of God and how much of the prophet himself. That is to say, we find ourselves acutely involved in the problems of discerning true and false prophecy. That, however, simply attests further to the reality of shared experience in charismatic/pentecostal and biblical traditions, for the same problem was as acute in both Old and New Testament times as it is today (cp. 1 Kings 13; 22; Matt. 7:22; 1 John 4:1).[7]

---

[7] The prophetic writings in the Bible have stood the test of time and have been fully recognised as authentically inspired of God in a way that is quite unique, and hence are accepted as sacred scripture. They do, however, still reveal the individual personalities of the prophets themselves in considerable measure.

CHAPTER FOUR

Shared Experience of the Life and Ministry of Jesus

Jesus replied, 'Let it be so now; it is proper for us to do this to fulfil all righteousness.'

(Matt. 3:15)

It is not only with prophets and apostles that the charismatic finds himself at home, but also with the man Jesus, who, because he was a man like us, had to be baptised and to receive the Holy Spirit. That may seem a strange statement to make about the incarnate Son of God, but one of the early effects of a charismatic's shared experience is to show him the complete humanity of Jesus, that he was indeed 'made like his brothers in every way' (Heb. 2:17). This conviction does not come through accepting some doctrine he is taught, as it does to many Christians, but through observation of how much Jesus' experience of the Spirit and his own have in common.

Receiving the Spirit—Jesus our Pattern

Among the Christological puzzles that confront many readers of the gospels are such questions as, 'If Jesus was the Son of God, why did he have no active ministry before the age of thirty?' and 'Why did he have to receive the Spirit of God at the Jordan before he entered on his ministry?' To most charismatics these are not pressing questions, for to them the early life of Jesus and the way his ministry began are illustrations of how God regularly operates with those who embark on ministry in the power of the Spirit. They will tell that, before they were baptised in the Spirit themselves, they were religious people, church-goers, believers in God and in Christ, but they will also recall how their faith was shrouded in doubt and puzzlement about the person of Christ, and even at times the very existence of God. They will also frequently confess to shallowness and frustration in their prayers, lack of enthusiasm for the Bible, and generally failure to see any evidence of the power of God at work in their lives. In other words, their God was more a belief or an idea than a living, personal being, and since he never actually seemed to do anything in their experience, they had nothing of much interest to tell about their Christianity, except how they had gone to Sunday school, then to church, and so forth. However, they will go on to add that after baptism in the Spirit all that changed. Life became more exciting, God became real, miracles and wonders began to happen, the Bible sprang to life, old doubts fled away, prayer became enjoyable and more purposeful, and Jesus stepped down from his remoteness to become an intimate friend.

The similarities with the early life of Jesus are unmistakable. Nothing of any great consequence, or at least nothing the gospel-writers thought worth recording, happened in his life before his baptism in the Holy Spirit. He simply grew up, a child of devout parents, growing 'in wisdom and stature, and in favour with God and men', as Luke 2:52 puts it. The story of his childhood visit to the Temple tells us little more than that he was a bright boy with an unusually acute appreciation of spiritual things and some awareness of his own destiny. We cannot, of course, draw the parallels too closely, for we never read of Jesus having some of the early problems we have, such as doctrinal problems, difficulties in understanding Scripture, lack of satisfaction in prayer, and the like. But what is most evident is his lack of power for ministry—so much so that later apocryphal gospels attempted to remedy this apparent deficiency in the four canonical gospels. However, the childhood stories they introduce are often so grotesque that they are clearly spurious and represent nothing more than the legendary inventions of pious imagination.

Then, just as for us today, so for Jesus everything changed when the Spirit of God descended on him at his baptism. The first and immediate effect was a vivid conviction, conveyed by the voice from heaven, of the Fatherhood of God ('You are my Son') and also an awareness of the

Father's love ('. . . whom I love; with you I am well pleased'). Most charismatics will give similar, though naturally never identical, accounts of their own first impressions, speaking of assurance, acceptance, knowledge of God's Fatherly love, etc. The parallel is very close.

But the similarities do not end at that initial stage; it is only there that they begin. Baptism in the Spirit is not just a flutter of spiritual excitement, but a life-transforming event and so is usually followed by a shorter or longer period of sometimes quite painful adjustment. Old ways that were not of God are jettisoned, new ways of the Spirit have to be learned, and the war between the Spirit and the flesh, as Paul calls it, now begins in earnest. It is by no means easy to give up those sins that have been accepted and even enjoyed for the past twenty, thirty, forty years, though many of them do instantly drop away without any struggle at all. Nor is it always a simple matter to accept that one is becoming the sort of religious enthusiast that one has hitherto viewed with suspicion, though there is a great deal of joy in it all. The temptation to withdraw from what is happening is strong, and accompanying it is a natural tendency to dismiss the baptism experience as something purely psychological. The early weeks of adjustment to the new life of the Spirit are usually fairly turbulent ones. And that also was how it was with Jesus. In the wilderness he was tempted to doubt his revelation. The voice had said, 'You are my son,' and the devil made that the focus of his scorn: 'If you are the Son of God,' . . . prove it: turn those stones into bread; try jumping from the top of the Temple! Or again: you're a fool to go pursuing this way of religious fanaticism; there's an easier way, the way everyone else takes to fame and fortune; let me give you the kingdoms of the world! The temptations are just like those we still have to face today after baptism in the Spirit. It took Jesus forty days to come to terms with his Spirit-baptism, but he emerged from his tussle 'in the power of the Spirit' (Luke 4:14) to begin the ministry that was to turn the world upside down. Sadly not all charismatics end with the same firm dedication he attained.

One of the first things a charismatic wants to do is tell his friends, and particularly the Christians at his local church, about the exciting thing that has happened to him, but more often than not he is met with either scorn or unbelief and can sometimes get quite upset about it. We see the same again with Jesus. When he went back to Nazareth and told them in his home synagogue: 'The Spirit of the Lord is on me . . . Today this scripture is fulfilled in your hearing,' his enthusiasm was not matched with the reception he got and so we watch him sadly walking from their midst saying, 'I tell you the truth, no prophet is accepted in his home town.' (Luke 4:18,21,24)

If the charismatic finds his old friends will not heed him, he equally discovers, like Jesus, that there are others who will. Quite quickly reports about his new-found blessing reach the ears of many in the neighbourhood who are impressed, or even captivated by what he has to say (cp. Luke 4:14,32). Then he realises that somehow he now knows what his faith is all about and can speak of it with a certainty and assuredness that must in some way be akin to the authority the ancients recognised in Jesus' teaching. And so, like Jesus, he finds himself being regularly sought out for advice and guidance about matters of faith.

He will also find that his new clarity of vision is accompanied by a startling appearance of miraculous activity. Prayers are answered in surprising ways, sick people are healed at a touch or with a word, others tell of personal blessings from being with him. He finds he is able to recognise degrees of faith in those with whom he converses, he seems to know by some kind of inner revelation what God wants him to do or say in particular circumstances, or what certain individuals need for their healing or blessing. His awareness of good and evil is heightened, he begins to distinguish between moral (good and evil) and spiritual (angelic and demonic) spheres of activity. Indeed he finds in these and so many other ways his experiences draw very close to the patterns discernible in the ministry of Jesus, his master.

Again, like Jesus he finds an inner urge to withdraw for prayer whenever possible. He becomes increasingly aware of a divine purpose for his life and of a growing desire to do the will of the Father above all else. There comes a recognition that his life-style is beginning to conform in greater measure to the pattern of Jesus', and with that a corresponding desire that it should continue to do so more and more. As he persists in this way, he discovers also that faith grows stronger and he is more resolute in his walk with God. The Jesus-pattern is now virtually indelible and the process towards total conformity of will becomes well nigh irreversible.

The conclusion is fairly obvious. Jesus is the Christian's pattern because he was the first New Testament charismatic himself. Because he was made like us in every respect (except that he did not sin; Heb. 2:17; 4:15), he shared, not only our physical limitations, but also our intellectual and spiritual limitations. He therefore needed to be filled with the Holy Spirit to enable him to do the works he could not have done by natural human means, to have the insight and understanding of God and men he could never have attained by natural intellectual processes and to have the constancy of will and purpose to enable him to conquer the world, the flesh and the devil by living the life of obedience in the face of circumstances that would have broken the natural human spirit. Jesus is the Christian's prophetic prototype.

Effects on Churchmanship and Scholarship

But there are other facets to shared experience besides these. The prophetic way is a very fulfilling and spiritually satisfying way, and so is one of great joy and consolation, as it was too for Jesus. But then it is also not the world's way, or, to use the language of John's Gospel, it is not loved by the world. So ultimately shared experience is also the way of rejection and the cross. But as Jesus encountered his strongest opposition among the religious of his day, so also the charismatic finds his first and most distressing opponents are other Christians. Hence the drumming out of the synagogues has its modern parallel in the flow of charismatics from the denominations into Pentecostal churches and other independent or 'house' churches.

Shared experience with Jesus such as this has obvious ramifications for biblical theology. The first of these is, of course, a loss of sympathy with liberal tendencies to explain away much of the miraculous in the gospels in terms of mythology, legend, psychology or whatever. But it becomes equally difficult to read the gospels with the view commonly held by conservative scholars that the miracles are only manifestations of Jesus' unique divinity. Indeed it is now easier to think of them as the typical actions of a charismatic, and so to view them as works performed in and through the power of the Holy Spirit. Hence it becomes needful to maintain that Jesus had to be endowed with this empowering of the Spirit in order to be able to perform them, as we too have to be. In fact, according to John's Gospel, where the miracles are regarded as 'signs' of Jesus' unique relationship with the Father, Jesus himself did not think of them solely in that way, nor did he even think of them as the ultimate in spiritual activity, for he taught his disciples that they would be able to do the same works themselves, and also greater works than he had done (John 14:12).

Likewise, shared experience is in proportion to faith, for charismatics do differ in the degree to which they share in the life and ministry of Jesus. None the less, the pattern is recognisable, however incomplete, and it radically alters a Christian's view of the gospels and of the person of Christ when he finds that, to whatever degree of equivalence, the things he does and says and experiences are also the things Jesus did and said and experienced. The standard by which he now measures the writings is no longer that of literalism, or of scientific criticism, but of his own experience. That, of course, must leave many questions unanswered, but it also makes the gospels so much more exciting, for every new day with the Spirit brings new revelations and events that shed light of some sort on those aspects of the gospels that still remain a mystery. Veritably the charismatic discovers that the best illuminator of Scripture is the Holy Spirit, who, as the Spirit of truth, leads us into all the truth.

CHAPTER FIVE

Shared Experience of Jesus as Lord

The gospel . . . regarding his Son, who as to his human nature was a descendant of David, and who through the Spirit of holiness was declared with power to be the Son of God by his resurrection from the dead: Jesus Christ our Lord.

(Rom. 1:2-4)

During his lifetime Jesus said many things to the disciples that they found hard to understand, mostly things about his own death and resurrection and about who he really was. They got occasional glimpses of the truth, such as when at Caesarea Pilippi Peter recognised Jesus as 'the Christ, the Son of the living God' (Matt. 16:16), or at the transfiguration when Peter and his companions heard the voice from heaven announce, 'This is my Son, whom I love' (Matt. 17:5), but these glimpses were not accompanied by any proper comprehension, as the sequel in both instances clearly shows. While the disciples recognised something in Jesus that attracted them, and sufficiently so to make them leave their employments to follow him, still they never properly understood him during his earthly life. They called him Master, Teacher and Prophet, but they felt no urge to worship him as Lord. They were prepared to follow him as Messiah and to wield their swords on his behalf, but it is doubtful that any of them even began to appreciate the full significance of the claim that he was the Son of God.

The Spirit Reveals Jesus as My Lord and My Saviour

The resurrection appearances, of course, must have made a great deal of difference to their thinking and understanding, but even in the stories about these events the disciples are still as men being taught, and still very puzzled. It is only after Pentecost that their puzzlement vanishes and is replaced by the sort of assurance and certainty that we saw in Jesus himself. The role of the disciples suddenly changes: no longer are they the pupils, but now the teachers. And their teaching is not in the nature of philosophical speculation about possible interpretations of the meaning of Jesus' life, death and resurrection, but in proclamation with authority that 'God has raised this Jesus to life . . . Exalted at the right hand of God . . . God has made this Jesus . . . both Lord and Christ' (Acts 2:32-6).

Charismatics usually say that a similar change has taken place in their own thinking. They will tell how their earlier uncertainty and lack of understanding about the two natures of Christ was removed after baptism in the Spirit—not that they are now able to explain the metaphysics of traditional Christology, but only to speak of their conviction, or rather certainty approximating to knowledge, that Jesus is Lord and God. There remains no question about the fact that Jesus is Lord, only about how to express that fact. In John's Gospel Jesus explains this change in terms of the Spirit's action: 'When the Counsellor comes, whom I will send to you from the Father, the Spirit of truth who goes out from the Father, he will testify about me . . . He will guide you into all truth . . . He will bring glory to me by taking from what is mine and making it known to you.' (15:26; 16:13f) The charismatic would heartily endorse such statements. He would deny that he worships Jesus as Lord because he learned to do so from a teacher, or from the creed, or some other doctrinal statement, but rather because the Holy Spirit has glorified Christ for him himself. In other words, he shares the apostles' experience of Jesus as Lord.

But there is still more. One recurrent problem for many a Christian is to understand how the death of Christ actually works his salvation. He may know some of the common theological explanations in terms of sacrifice for sin, atonement, vicarious suffering, etc., but to him these are often just theories he finds difficult to grasp. Similarly traditional teaching about the resurrection tells him that because one man died and rose again, death has lost its grip on humanity, but that too is often little more than theory to him and he finds it difficult to understand its practical value for his life as a Christian. The ascension creates even greater problems and is usually conveniently forgotten, while Pentecost is commonly regarded as just something that happened a long time ago to get the Church started.

One of the effects of baptism in the Spirit is to internalise all these events or make them somehow a living part of my experience. The charismatic will feel that when Paul wrote about us dying and rising with Christ (Rom. 6:1-11), he was not just explaining the meaning of sacramental baptism, but was speaking of an internally experiencable event. Baptism in the Holy Spirit so alters a person's life, rooting out old sins, killing off old fleshly desires, banishing old doubts and fears, and filling him with new joy and hope in believing, that he knows Christ's death and resurrection have now become his own, that he has experienced some kind of passage from death to life, or that he has already risen with Christ to eternal life. Paul elsewhere explains that this is an inner truth taught us by the Spirit whom God has given us as a guarantee of its validity (2 Cor. 4:16 - 5:5).

Just as Jesus is the New Testament prototype charismatic, so also he is the pioneer of resurrection; and just as I know him to be the prophet through my shared experience with him in the activities of the Holy Spirit, so also I know him to be risen and alive through my shared experience with him of death to an old life and of birth to a new life that is given me through the action of that same Spirit. Of course, for me this experience, as Paul says, is but in foretaste of a fuller glory and release, but it is real, none the less, and its very reality convinces me even more of the truth of the biblical assertions about Jesus' resurrection.

Above all, however, the Spirit shows us Christ in glory, the ascended Lord seated at God's right hand. Charismatics sometimes say that before their baptism in the Spirit theirs was a Christianity of the crucifix, but that it is now of the glorified Christ; or that they had a Lenten faith, but now it is an Easter faith, or an Ascension faith. Prophetic visions tend to be predominantly of Christ in glory and the prophecies are usually utterances of Christ the King.

Jesus, His Father, the Spirit and Me

Once we see Christ so highly exalted we come face to face with the Trinitarian problem of defining the relationship between the persons of the Godhead. But this also is a question the charismatic would want to approach in the light of his experience and of his observation of continuing activity of the Spirit in the Church. That, however, is an approach that can be rather untidy, unlike the carefully philosophical one adopted by those who formulated our creeds. It can leave many blurred edges and even an impression of confusion in the use of terminology. Thus the charismatic will say with equal facility and no sense of contradiction that it is now God, now Christ, or now the Spirit that speaks in his prophecies. But the same confusion equally exists in the New Testament itself.

During his lifetime Jesus taught and acted in the power of the Spirit of God and he prepared his disciples to continue his teaching and action in the power of that same Spirit, which he therefore promised would be given them once his own earthly ministry was accomplished. The activity of the Spirit in the disciples was therefore to make their ministry a continuation of Jesus' own. Hence Luke tells us in Acts 1:1 that his Gospel was only an account of what 'Jesus began to do and teach', the implication being that Acts is the record of what he continued to do and teach through the apostles by the action of the Spirit. John also sees continuity between the work of Jesus and the Spirit, for in 14:16 the Spirit is called 'a second Paraclete' (NIV 'another Counsellor'), while in 1 John 2:1 Jesus himself is called 'a Paraclete' (NIV 'one who speaks in our defence', AV 'advocate'; cp. Isa. 9:6 where Messiah is called 'Counsellor'). In a similar way Paul in Rom. 8:9-11 happily uses the expressions 'the Spirit of God', 'the Spirit of Christ' and 'Christ' interchangeably. In Acts 16:7 Luke even uses the expression 'the Spirit of Jesus'. While this merging or identification of the roles of the Spirit and Christ may create a few problems for the theologian who might prefer more precise doctrinal definition, it raises few practical problems for the charismatic who naturally speaks the same language anyhow without feeling any need to be more carefully analytical than the New Testament authors were. It is again part of his shared experience with the apostles.

Even though the charismatic may fail to distinguish consistently between the actions of the Spirit and of Christ in daily experience, he does share the New Testament belief that Christ is the one who baptises with the Holy Spirit. John the Baptist said he would have this function, but it was not one Jesus actually exercised during his earthly life, because during 'that time the Spirit had not been given, since Jesus had not yet been glorified' (John 7:37-9). It was not Jesus the charismatic who gave the Spirit, but Jesus the risen and ascended Lord. Peter explained it thus in his Pentecost sermon: 'Exalted to the right hand of God, he (Jesus) has received from the Father the promised Holy Spirit and has poured out what you now see and hear.' (Acts 2:33)

Putting these two observations together, that Jesus still acts by his Spirit and that he is the one who baptises with the Spirit, the charismatic teaches that all who would be his disciples today must receive the Spirit from him in the same sort of way as his first disciples did. He therefore happily endorses John the Baptist's distinction between water-baptism and Spirit-baptism and insists that, while the former is required by our Lord's command, the latter is just as essential for any who would follow in his footsteps.

This emphasis on the need for Spirit baptism causes the most heated debates between charismatics and non-charismatics. We do not need to get caught up in that debate here, only to note that the charismatic bases his interpretation of John the Baptist's teaching, and indeed of various other corroborative passages in John, Acts and Paul, on his own personal experience, which is thus again shown to be part of his shared experience with the New Testament writers.

Implications for Biblical Interpretation

Various corollaries depend on these observations. If a charismatic acts in the power of the same Spirit as Christ's, then his charismata or gifts ought to be at least similar to Jesus' own. More than that, if such close identity between Christ and the Spirit as we have noted in the New Testament writings exists in the one Godhead, and if 'Jesus Christ is the same yesterday and today and for ever' (Heb. 13:8), then prophecies spoken by present-day charismatics must sometimes be in some measure the words of Christ. Now there is a whole area of New Testament scholarship that seeks to distinguish between authentic sayings of the historical Jesus and words that might have been originally prophetic words uttered in his name by early Christians, but preserved in the New Testament as if they were spoken by him directly. This field of study is highly speculative and one that fortunately we need not become involved in here, but merely noting its existence again highlights an aspect of contemporary belief that overlaps with it. In harmony with Scripture which acknowledges Jesus, not only as Priest, King and Lord, but also as Prophet, charismatics hold that, though ascended to the heavens, he is still also Prophet today, and still speaks through Spirit-filled believers in much the same way as he spoke through his earliest followers.

This observation is as important for understanding a charismatic's interpretation of the Old Testament as of the New. If Christian prophecy is the voice of the Spirit glorifying Christ (John 16:14), or is even the voice of Christ himself, then it must be that that same Spirit which spoke through the prophets of the Old Testament was also the Spirit of Jesus Christ who is the same yesterday, etc. In other words, the old fashioned idea that the Old Testament prophets spoke of Christ or that Christ himself spoke in the Old Testament is one that charismatics would find no difficulty in holding, for as we have seen, they feel a strong affinity with the Old Testament prophets and believe that the same Spirit inspired them also. Of course there was a difference between the pre-Christian and the Christian prophets, but we shall deal with that more

Shared Experience of Jesus as Lord

fully in Chapter Eight. Here it is enough to note that as Christian prophets speak to glorify the work of Jesus in the past, or to utter his words today, so Old Testament prophets spoke to prepare for his future work, or to utter his words in their own day.

It is the charismatic's shared experience, not only with the apostles but also with the prophets, that confirms him unshakeably in belief in the pre-existence of Christ, and he should therefore find himself in heart-felt agreement with the doctrines and sentiments expressed by Paul in such well-known Christological hymns to the eternal lordship of Jesus as we find in Phil. 2 or Col. 1. However, he would also have to admit that his shared experience of the divine Christ would only enable him to proclaim his conviction or to compose hymns of praise in his honour, as the early Christians did, but not to explain his Christological beliefs to the satisfaction of a philosophical theologian. But then the New Testament Christians did not write philosophical theology either, and that negative observation in itself also reflects an aspect of the New Testament experience that charismatics today tend to share.

The fact that charismatics are usually better at declaring their belief in Christ as Lord than at explaining it has sometimes created an impression of anti-intellectualism. And certainly it must be admitted that, whether Paul and other New Testament writers were warning against becoming involved in disputes with Gnostic heretics or not, those passages where they advise their readers to avoid philosophy, or what is falsely called knowledge, or controversies, or dissensions (e.g. Col. 2:8; 1 Tim. 6:3; Tit. 3:9), do have a strange appeal to charismatics who often see no need to pass beyond declaration of belief into speculation about it. The reasons for this attitude will become clearer later, but in the meantime it is enough to note that charismatics, like the New Testament Christians, are better at proclaiming and hymning Jesus as Lord that an explaining his Lordship, and also that they believe their desire so to preach and sing comes from the same Spirit of Christ dwelling in them as was in the early apostles—in other words, that they believe that they too share in the biblical experience of Jesus as Lord.

CHAPTER SIX

Shared Experience of God as Father

Because you are sons, God sent the Spirit of his Son into our hearts, the Spirit who calls out, 'Abba, Father.'

(Gal. 4:6)

When the Holy Spirit descended on Jesus at the Jordan, he received from his heavenly Father an unforgettable assurance of his sonship, and it was on that revelation that the wilderness temptations mainly focused. Yet while there is therefore no doubt that Jesus was fully aware of his sonship, there is little evidence, in the first three gospels at any rate, that he actually spoke much about it. It was recognised by demons (cp. Mark 3:11), according to Matthew's account it was disclosed to Peter at Caesarea Philippi (Matt 16:16), and then at the Transfiguration it was affirmed to three of the disciples by the voice from heaven (Mark 9:7). But Jesus mentions it himself only twice (Matt. 11:27 = Luke 10:22, and Mark 13:32) and he binds the demons to silence about it (Mark 3:12). And so it seems his sonship was more part of his personal consciousness than of his teaching.

Receiving the Spirit of Sonship

When we think of it that way, we discover his consciousness was of a relationship that was warm and intimate. At the beginning of his ministry the voice at the baptism spoke of 'my Son, whom I love' and at the end, in Gethsemane, we hear him speak to God with the familiar title a Jewish child would use with its natural father, '*Abba*' (Mark 14:36), the title preachers delight to translate, 'Daddy'. The same closeness is very much highlighted in the fourth Gospel where Jesus speaks more openly of it, for example in John 17, where great emphasis is laid on the

Father's and the Son's love for each other and their mutual indwelling or mystical union.

Now it is clear from both the Synoptics and John that Jesus did not simply regard this warm consciousness as his own unique preserve, but expected his disciples to share something of it. The simple opening to the Lord's Prayer in Luke 11—'Father' instead of the longer 'Our Father' in Matt. 6:9—suggests Jesus may have taught his disciples to use the expression, *Abba*, themselves. The Christian's place in this son/Father-relationship is even more clearly defined in John's Gospel. We read about it first in his prologue: 'to all who received him, to those who believed in his name, he gave the right to become children of God' (John 1:12). In chapter 17, where Jesus speaks much of the Father's love for him, he prays all converts will share in that same love-relationship as he himself enjoys (17:20,23,26). Earlier, in his conversation with Nicodemus he speaks of the believer's relationship with God resulting from a new birth, from being 'born again . . . of water and the Spirit' (3:1-15). In doing so he lays more emphasis on the Spirit (mentioned three times, in vv. 5,6,8) than on water (only once, in v.5), but the fact that he speaks of both puts us sharply in mind of his own baptism, when the Spirit came upon him and he himself entered into the fullest assurance of his Sonship. And that, says the charismatic, is the pattern that should be common to us all in our own Christian experience as well—a new birth through the action of the Holy Spirit in which we receive a profound assurance that God is our loving heavenly Father too.

The link between the Spirit and sonship is perhaps more clearly defined by Paul who, in the quotation at the head of this chapter and in the parallel passage in Rom. 8:15f, speaks about Christians in the Spirit crying '*Abba*, Father', just like Jesus. When we do that, he says in Rom. 8, 'The Spirit himself testifies with our spirit that we are God's children.' Commentators have discussed whether Paul was referring to some liturgical formula, or some confession of faith in God as Father, or the beginning of the Lord's Prayer, but the charismatic will ardently maintain that he was more probably thinking about a profound and spontaneous cry from the heart that results from baptism in the Holy Spirit. The New Testament conviction, he will argue, that God is a personal Father (not just the national Father of the Old Testament or the global Father of some popular and Church thinking) is something taught by the Spirit, first to Jesus himself, and then through shared experience, to all who are born of the Spirit. In the same way as it was part of Jesus' living self-consciousness, not just of his teaching, so also it should be part of our experience rather than simply of our doctrine. The really worthwhile articulation is not the theological statement that God is Father, but that heart-felt cry of the loved child, '*Abba*', which is generally as much part of the experience of today's charismatic as it was of Paul and his contemporaries.

Implications for Personal Faith and Experience

Recognition that the Fatherhood of God is as much experiential as doctrinal for the charismatic helps us to understand some other aspects of his shared experience. His '*Abba*, Father', uttered in response to his new awareness of God's warm, protecting love, is essentially a cry of joyous praise, and joyous praise has been very much a hallmark of the Charismatic Movement. It finds its natural outlet in song rather than in theological treatise, which perhaps explains why charismatics, while some of them are engaged in the task of theological reflection, tend on the whole to express their faith more through the medium of hymns and spiritual songs. But then prophets and mystics in every age have demonstrated a strong propensity towards hymn-writing and poetic expression. Much of Old Testament prophecy is in verse form, and some scholars believe that a number of the psalms in the Psalter were written by prophets. Today's charismatic and revival movements are producing an endless flow of new songs, and significantly the majority of these are songs of praise and joy. The prophet and the mystic may know much of suffering and rejection, but in the presence of God they find that joyful praise is their most natural expression.

There are parallels in the Old Testament, such as in the Book of Habakkuk, where the prophet gives vent to song about his glorious vision of God, even though he is perturbed about the suffering in his society, or in Ps. 73 where we find one of the warmest expressions of devotion and praise on the lips of a man who is clearly distressed by his own suffering which contrasts so vividly with the prosperity of the godless. Hence we find that today's charismatic responds readily and eagerly to such praise-filled passages in the Bible as Rom. 8, Ephes. 1-3, Col. 1, or the hymns scattered through Revelation. Likewise, he will tell how he appreciates Paul's injunction to 'Rejoice in the Lord always' (Phil. 4:4), or to 'give thanks in all circumstances' (1 Thes. 5:18). It is in fact such passages as these that provide the raw material for many of the popular songs currently being produced.

Praise among charismatics and in the Bible is not only directed to God as Father, but also to God as King, to the victorious creator and sustainer of the universe. However, the charismatic's understanding of God's Kingship is very closely related to his appreciation of God's Fatherhood, because its focus is every bit as much the lives of his subjects as the stars of heaven or the waves of the sea. It certainly does have a cosmic dimension, but that too centres on the charismatic's own experience of God in the Spirit. For example, he might speak of a sense of being taken up into the structure and purpose of the universe, or of a sense of unity and harmony in and with things in heaven and earth. These are perhaps the sort of awarenesses we associate more readily with mystics, but Paul apparently knew something of such matters (2 Cor. 12: 1-7; Ephes. 1:3-10), and they remain a fairly regular aspect of contemporary prophetic experience.

There is a realisation that the world is not just a random arrangement of atoms and molecules, but a coherent, purposeful structure, and that I am part of it. God has a place and purpose for me in it, and I realise my part in his design as I adhere to the Christ through whom it is revealed to me. Paul uses the word '(pre)destined' in Ephes. 1:5; current jargon is 'God's perfect plan for my life', but neither terminology should be taken to imply a doctrine of determinism in the traditional sense. Prophetic faith tends to have little sympathy with the inflexibility of doctrinalism, and anyhow Paul himself speaks of something that is 'made known' (Ephes. 1:9), while the charismatic will most likely talk about 'being shown' or 'being led' by the Spirit. The corresponding language of Jesus was that of the will and obedience, of seeking 'to do the will of him who sent me' (John 4:34; 5:30; 6:38f). But even Jesus was only shown that will and had to 'learn obedience' to it, as Heb. 5:8 puts is (cp. Mark 14:36). Hence the charismatic, while he shares with Jesus and the early Christians that sense of God's Fatherhood that evokes his praise of God as King, he also shares with them that call to obedient submission to God his heavenly Father as God his King.

Basically these two responses are reflections of an awareness of God's protecting love and also of his having a specific purpose and intention for my life. Just as the awareness of the former comes from the activity of the Spirit in showing us the Father, so also the latter derives from the experience of being 'marked with a seal, the promised Holy Spirit' (Ephes. 1:13). The life of the charismatic is by no means simply one of exuberant praise; it is also one of radical obedience to the Spirit's revelation. Again it is significant that awareness of God's Kingship is asserted more through experience of God in the Spirit than through doctrine or theology. Hence its expression, like that of God's Fatherhood, is found more in the praises and life-style of the charismatic than anywhere else, and so belongs for him most properly in the category of shared experience.

Implications for Biblical Interpretation

The significance of these observations for the charismatic's view of biblical interpretation is again striking. It becomes difficult for him to read those parts of the Bible that speak of God as Father as though they only contained expressions of any particular writer's ideas or opinions about God, for he finds himself recognising familiar experiences of God that he has had too recorded or echoed in them. The Holy Spirit has so lifted him into the Father's love and purpose, to be there with Christ, to share in his sonship and obedience, that he finds himself living in Jesus' and the apostles' experiences of God. He will share in the praises of Paul, or in Jesus' love for the Father much more readily than he will want to analyse or question the passages that speak of those things.

And finally, he will find it as difficult to have doubts any more about the existence of God as he would about the divine Sonship of Jesus, for that too is confirmed to him by the Spirit, or as John puts it, 'God lives in him and he in God' and 'We know that we live in him and he in us, because he has given us of his Spirit' (1 John 4:15,13). Note that John says 'know', not just 'believe' or 'trust'. The charismatic would use equally strong language, but we have seen before how the Spirit takes belief and turns it into knowledge. John expresses it slightly differently earlier in his letter: 'As for you, the anointing you received from him remains in you, and you do not need anyone to teach you. But as his anointing teaches you about all things and as that anointing is real, not counterfeit—just as it has taught you, remain in him.' (1 John 2:27) No charismatic would feel at home with the kind of biblical interpretation that speaks simply of 'the supernatural', 'the divine', 'the numinous', 'the transcendent', or that would seek to interpret all in terms of purely human understanding, scientific thought, or philosophy. To him God is Father, Lord and King, and is very near and very personal. Prophetic talk is God-talk, as also, of course, is Bible talk.

CHAPTER SEVEN

The Bible as Prophetic Literature

In the past God spoke to our forefathers through the prophets at many times and in various ways, but in these last days he has spoken to us by his Son.

(Heb. 1:1-2)

All charismatics are convinced of this, that in some way or other God does actually speak to people, whether to individuals, church groups, whole congregations, or even to some in the wider non-church community, through visions, auditions, prophecies, dreams, or 'in various ways', as Hebrews puts it, but certainly that he does speak. And so they find no need to dismiss as merely legendary the stories of God's conversations and communications with Abraham, Moses, Samuel, Solomon, Peter, Paul, or whoever. From their own experience and their conversations with other Spirit-filled Christians they know that such things are not uncommon, and so they view the literature that tells of them somewhat differently from the liberal scholar who would tend to use words like 'myth' or 'legend' in his discussions about it. The expression I myself prefer is 'prophetic (or charismatic) literature', because the biblical books are often very similar to the sort of writing we find in contemporary charismatic (auto)biographies, accounts of church renewal, records of healing and revival ministries and the like, of which there are plentiful examples in our bookshops today.

It is clearly impossible to discuss all the books in the Bible here[8], or to maintain that they all contain the same level of charismatic literature, though it is surprising how much of it one finds in the most unexpected places, such as in Numbers, or Deuteronomy, or Proverbs, or Song of

---

[8] Fully discussed in *The Way of the Spirit*.

Songs, or 2 Chronicles, or Ezra and Nehemiah. Our task here must be more circumscribed, to deal only with a representative selection and to show how a charismatic's approach should lend itself to new and different ways of understanding the biblical books.

The Old Testament

Let us start at the beginning, with *Genesis*. Here we read many times about the patriarchs having conversations with God. Liberal scholars would generally dismiss these conversations as little more than the literary technique of the ancient narrative writer without seeing any need to think of them as in any way reflections of what might have happened. Conservatives, by contrast, would say they did actually take place that way, word for word, though of course we cannot properly appreciate how, since we have nothing today with which to compare them. Both liberals and conservatives might argue, from their very different standpoints, that such conversations, or the records of them at any rate, belong to a fairly primitive stage of religious development, and that God has more refined ways of communicating with us now.

If you look at almost any pentecostal biography, you will find stories that are very similar, of men who, like Abraham, gave up known securities to embark on lives of ministry or mission because God told them to do so, and who were sustained in their ministries by further confirmations of a similar nature. The communications are sometimes of a Joan-of-Arc sort, the hearing of an audible voice, sometimes of a more visionary kind in which the conversation has a rather dream-like quality, sometimes of a more intuitive nature, with a kind of inner voice speaking in the soul, but always the claim is the same, that there is a clear and definite directive from God to the believer.

Now, care must be taken to distinguish prophetic literature of this sort from other literature that speaks of psychic communications. As in Genesis, so also in the charismatic biography, God speaks of himself and of what brings his purposes to fruition, whether in the life of an individual or in a church community. When he speaks of his will for a believer, he may speak with words of guidance, exhortation or promise, as in the commission to Abraham to go from his home to the land God would show him, or as in the promise to bless him and mediate blessing through him to others (Gen. 12:1-3), or even as in the more specific guidance he gave to the servant sent to choose Isaac's wife (Gen. 24). God's conversations with the Christian, as with the partriarchs, are never in the nature of mere idle conversation about purely private matters, but are always somehow related to his purpose for a church or community and to the better implementation of the gospel in the lives of his people. Thus they are generally words that hold out a challenge to faith, that speak of an objective, that lead somewhere, such as to the creation of a revived church, much as God's words to Abraham led to the creation of a new people, Israel.

The charismatic feels very much at home in this sort of literature, but while he cannot sympathise with liberal incredulity about it, he may also balk at conservative dogmatism. To him the Genesis narratives are first and foremost stories about men's responses in faith, or lack of it, to what they knew God was asking them to do. Strange as it may seem, the literal precision of God's words is not normally a matter of great concern to him—it is not too often he can be so sure of the verbal accuracy of his own communications either. What is important, however, is the message, its meaning, its intention, and also how the one who receives it responds to it. The main delight in these stories, both in Genesis and today, lies not just in their recounting of divine speeches, but in their portrayals of strength and weaknesses of faith in their leading personalities, in their tales of success and failure, in their accounts of how others have fared in responding to God's call. From them we learn much about how we ourselves either promote or hamper God's will. And the yardstick is always faith, never the letter—but more about that in the next chapter.

It is important to note in passing that analogies with contemporary pentecostal experience cannot be used to confirm the historicity of biblical narratives such as these. It certainly adds a sense of greater plausibility to them, but in the end of the day it can do no more than encourage a more sympathetic reading than many scholars would care to allow. Questions of historicity must be established on grounds other than the recognition that Abraham's experiences are of a sort that I can understand and appreciate because they are so similar to my own. That recognition only tells me what sort of literature I am reading, not whether the events it recounts actually happened in the way it describes.

Many of the incidents in the life of *Moses* are of the same sort as those in the partriarchal stories, but he also had a more startling encounter with God on Mount Sinai, which by any standards must be regarded as quite unique. I know of nothing comparable in charismatic experience, but even in the Bible itself the Sinai revelation is unparalleled. None the less, to the charismatic there is something recognisable about Moses' awareness of the terrible majesty of God, or the radiance of his face when he descended the mountain, or his reluctance to accept his commission, or the super-human boldness with which he confronted Pharaoh, or the anguish he experienced in the face of his people's lack of understanding and their rejection of his leadership. The biography of Moses, despite the uniqueness of the Sinai story, contains many elements not unlike those found in the biographies of today's charismatic leaders.

The book of *Judges* is full of stories about charismatics. These were men on whom the Spirit rested and who led Israel's armies in the power of the Spirit to victory over invading oppressors. Again there are no good parallels in contemporary literature, because the present-day Charismatic Movement is not military except in a spiritual sense. There are, however, plenty of excellent parallels in the literature of the Camisards, a prophetic/charismatic movement in Southern France at the turn of the seventeenth-eighteenth centuries that inspired persecuted Protestants to a guerrilla-style resistance against the oppression of Catholic troops. Nevertheless, the modern pentecostal reader finds himself very much at home with someone like Gideon, who put out his

The Bible as Prophetic Literature

fleece before God and who led his little, devoted band into battle in faith, and he will even find in the Samson stories salutary lessons about how a charismatic ought not to live his life.

When we come to *1 Samuel* we find ourselves reading a book that is really very like a modern charismatic biography in places. Typically the story is set in a context of moral and political decadence, which is highlighted by the behaviour of the priests at the sanctuary at Shiloh. The need for revival is evident, but 'In those days,' we are told, 'the word of the LORD was rare' (3:1). Our hope is focused on the hero, Samuel, but he, though from a devout home, was being trained by a priest who had a pretty ineffectual ministry. Then comes the account of Samuel's night vision, which takes the place of the charismatic's baptism in the Spirit story, and from that point 'Samuel was attested as a prophet of the LORD' (3:20). We only get a few glimpses of his ministry, but from them we discover that he became the leader of a revival that swept through the land (cp. 3:19 - 4:1;7:3-17), and that he became something of a national figurehead. But more important for our purposes, we discover that he became the head of a prophetic movement, something like the equivalent of a modern charismatic church (10:5-13; 19:18-24), and that it was through the activity of this prophetic group that Saul, the first king of Israel, became himself a charismatic. As the story continues Saul and Samuel separated and Saul's spiritual endowment went sour. In the end we find him seeking guidance from a witch, in desperation that God no longer speaks to him. Tension between prophetic Christianity and spiritualist or magical arts is again a common feature in modern literature. 1 Samuel breathes a very contemporary atmosphere to the charismatic. Again he sits apart form the liberal and the conservative in his view of it.

2 Samuel and *1 & 2 Kings* contain many sections that are delightfully appealing to charismatics, such as the story of the confounding of Ahithophel's wisdom in response to David's prayer (1 Sam. 15:30 - 17:23), or the account of Solomon's enduement with the gift of wisdom after his vigil of prayer at the Gibeon sanctuary (1 Kings 3:3-28), and in particular the many prophet stories that are found scattered through 1 Kings 11 - 2 Kings 20. The miraculous provision of food for Elijah (1 Kings 17), the effectiveness of his prayer in confounding the Baal prophets (ch. 18), his loss of nerve, flight and restitution through an encounter with God (ch. 19), the call and empowering of Elisha (19:19-21; 2 Kings 2:9-16), the confrontation of true and false prophet (1 Kings 22), and the catalogue of miracles and wonders in 2 Kings 2-9 are characteristic of the kind of events and narratives with which the modern literature abounds and in which charismatics take a great deal of pleasure. Of course some will say that in the retelling there could sometimes have been a tendency to heighten their dramatic appeal, but these tales are not for that reason to be dismissed as mere legends, as liberals maintain. They have a ring of essential truth when measured by the rule of shared experience.

Job is a book that some might be surprised to find included in this chapter, but to my mind it is one of the best examples of charismatic literature in the Old Testament, indeed one that deals with precisely the kind of tensions we are discussing here. Job's conversation with his theologically minded friends might be compared with a lot of our present-day discussion about the problem of suffering. It considers solutions that the various speakers hold to be satisfying in some sense, at least at a philosophical level, but which the stark reality of Job's need shows to be lacking in either satisfactoriness or usefulness. After some thirty chapters of such tedious debate, which gets nowhere except deeper into frustration and despair, an eager, though embarrassed young man called Elihu steps forward (ch. 32). He is embarrassed because he feels like a young student speaking in the presence of mature, theological experts (32:6), but he claims a wisdom and confidence that they seem to lack, saying, 'It is the Spirit in a man, the breath of the Almighty, that gives him understanding. For I am full of words, and the spirit within me compels me.' (32:8,18) Here is one who indeed speaks like a charismatic, and as he speaks on, not debating but preaching, his words, unlike those of Job's older friends, become increasingly full of God-talk that is praise-orientated. He, as it were, brings Job into God's presence and the end of his speech in ch. 37 passes almost imperceptibly into the words of God himself, for God continues it by saying the same things that Elihu had led Job to consider, about the majesty of the Creator. Elihu's words are like a bridge that carries us from theological debate which leads nowhere to praise that leads directly into God's healing presence. Job's final confession acknowledges the transition: 'My ears had heard of you (= theology), but now my eyes have seen you (= experience).' (42:5)

The book of Job is an excellent example of charismatic ministry in action. It highlights many of the tensions that exist between theological debate and experiential religion, and it has many contemporary counterparts, particularly in the records of healing ministries which operate very often through theologically inexperienced persons who show an aptitude for directing sufferers away form themselves and their problems to God. It should be noted in passing that liberal scholars regularly recommend omitting the Elihu speeches from the book as of little value; theological disputation is their forte anyhow. Conservatives, while they would not take such drastic action, nevertheless still tend to see Elihu's speeches as simply repeating the arguments of the other three counsellors, adding little to the philosophical arguments of the debate, and therefore of no special significance in the wider context of the book as a whole.

The book of *Psalms* is made up of so many different kinds of songs and hymns that it cannot be discussed in any detail here. What was written about it and about hymn-writing in general in the last chapter must suffice for the moment to show how much the charismatic will feel at home in the praise-dominated language of its worship.[9]

---

[9] See further J.W. McKay, 'The Experiences of Dereliction and of God's Presence in the Psalms; An exercise in Old Testament Exegesis in the Light of Renewal Theology', in *Faces of Renewal. Studies in honor of Stanley M. Horton*, edited by

Likewise, the book of *Proverbs* is a very mixed collection of sayings and covers too wide a variety of material for us to discuss here. At a general level it is worth remarking that wisdom, which is the main subject of the book, is one of the gifts of the Spirit listed by Paul in 1 Cor. 12. In various places Proverbs indicates that such wisdom is something given by God to those who have 'the fear of the LORD' (cp. 1:7) and who set themselves to seek it earnestly from him (3:13-18; 8:1 - 9:12), which again brings us into the realms of the experiential rather than the intellectual. And with that the charismatic is very much at home, with the expectation that God can give such wisdom, as he gave to Solomon, or as James says he will give to any who ask for it believing (1 Kings 3; James 1:5f).[10]

Space prohibits a more exhaustive study of the Old Testament. *The prophetic books* hardly need any comment, for they are unquestionably charismatic literature, or at least to the charismatic they are. Collections of prophetic utterances are not commonly found in print today, but the exiled Camisards in London and their English converts at the beginning of the eighteenth century published many such books which they entitled *Prophetical Warnings*. However, the present-day charismatic has heard and probably uttered many a prophecy himself and so from his experience of the spoken word recognises the literary category instantly. Since I have already discussed at the end of chapter two how a charismatic's view of prophecy differs from that of the liberal or the conservative, there is no need to say more on the subject at this point.[11]

P. Elbert, Hendrickson Publishers, Massachussetts, 1988. Also ibid, 'My Glory - A Mantle of Praise', *Scottish Journal of Theology* 31, 1978, pp. 167-72; 'Psalms of Vigil', *Zeitschrift für die alttestamentliche Wissenschaft* 91, 1979, pp. 229-47.

[10] See further J. McKay, *My Lord and My God*, The Way of the Spirit vol. 4, pp. 77f, 185-8.

[11] See further, J.W. McKay, 'The Old Testament and Christian Charismatic /Prophetic Literature', in *Scripture: Method and Meaning, Essays presented to Anthony Tyrrell Hanson*, edited by B.P. Thompson, Hull University Press, 1987.

The Bible as Prophetic Literature

The New Testament

The New Testament presents fewer problems in this context than the Old. From what has already been written in chapters two to six, it will be clear that *the synoptic Gospels* can be read like charismatic biographies, particularly Luke's, where a greater emphasis is put on the action of the Spirit in the initiation of Jesus' ministry (4:1-30), on his and his followers' experiences of joy in the Spirit (cp. 10:17,21), on prayer (cp. 6:12), and on teaching to prepare the disciples for receiving the Spirit themselves (11:1-13; 24:49). *John's Gospel* is also very full of teaching about the Spirit and about the Christian's need to receive him, particularly in chs. 3-7 and 14-16.

Acts, especially in the first half, is replete with charismatic hero stories, tales of outpourings of the Spirit, of healings and other miracles, of visions, of praise and rejoicing, of power-filled ministries, of divine guidance. It is not without reason that this book has sometimes been nicknamed 'the Acts of the Holy Spirit'.

Most of *Paul's letters* contain teaching about life in the spirit. He claims that his own understanding of Christianity, or his gospel, came to him by revelation from God, not by natural human processes (Gal. 1:12). He also speaks of the miracles that accompanied his preaching and gives the impression that he believed they were probably more effective in bringing his hearers to belief than his spoken words were (1 Cor. 2:1-5; Gal. 3:1-5). He tells that he speaks freely in tongues, that he prophesies, and that he estimates both these gifts very highly indeed (1 Cor. 14:1-5,18f). He encourages his readers not to quench the Spirit and not to despise prophesying (1 Thes. 5:19f). And in the progression of the argument of the letter to the Romans, he regards life in the Spirit as the full flowering of a Christian's faith (ch. 8). Even in the pastoral letters, which some scholars think were not written by Paul himself, Timothy is urged not to neglect the gift he received by prophetic utterance and the laying on of hands (1 Tim. 4:14) and to rekindle the gift that is in him (2

Tim. 1:6), while Titus is urged to 'stress' salvation 'through the washing of rebirth and renewal by the Holy Spirit' (Tit. 3:5-8).

The author of *Hebrews* tells how the gospel first came to his congregation accompanied by 'signs, wonders and various miracles, and gifts of the Holy Spirit' (2:4). *James* gives instruction for receiving God's wisdom (1:5f) and for ministry for healing the sick (5:13-15). *1 Peter* speaks of Christians 'filled with an inexpressible and glorious joy' (1:8) and *2 Peter* has some advice about the nature of prophetic inspiration (1:20f). *1 John* is full of teaching about the indwelling and abiding of God through the Holy Spirit (cp. 3:24), and even the little letter of *Jude* instructs its readers to pray in the Holy Spirit (v. 20).

Finally, *Revelation* is the only book in the New Testament that actually calls itself 'prophecy' (1:3; 22:7,10,18). It was written about a visionary experience of the author when he was 'in the Spirit' on one occasion (1:10) and is certainly to be described as prophetic literature. It could almost be said that every single book in the New Testament is about some aspect of life in the Spirit. There is scarcely a chapter in it where the charismatic does not find echoes of things he might want to say about his own experience of life in the Spirit or of things that other charismatics have told, whether in print or by word of mouth, about their experiences.

There is little doubt in my mind that the majority of the books of the Bible, in both testaments, are, in their very different ways and to different degrees, classifiable under the general umbrella-title of prophetic or charismatic literature. But if that can be said about individual books, how far can it be said about the Bible as a whole? It is to that question we must now address ourselves.

CHAPTER EIGHT

The Drama of Salvation

or

Creating the End-time Church of the Spirit

And afterward,
  I will pour out my Spirit on all people.
Your sons and daughters will prophesy,
  your old men will dream dreams,
  your young men will see visions.
Even on my servants, both men and women,
  I will pour out my Spirit in those days.

(Joel 2:28f)

One of the major problems to which biblical scholars of all shades of persuasion repeatedly address themselves is that of determining the theological theme that gives the Bible its unity and coherence. The suggested solutions have been many and varied, for example, that the central theme is that of covenant, or the kingdom of God, or the history of salvation. The debate continues. Some believe it will never be resolved. Others say the Bible has no consistent theological theme at all, but only many varied strands, and so they speak of diversity in the Bible rather than unity. They maintain there is no need to look for a common theological interest in such different materials as laws of sacrifice, prophetic utterances, hymns of praise, wisdom sayings, historical narratives, etc. Perhaps this question of theological unity will never be resolved, but it is my belief that there is a coherence, though it is one that I should prefer to call experiential or prophetic rather than academic or theological, and I believe this coherence can be grasped when we view the biblical records in the light of shared experience.

Since the theme we shall be reviewing is experiential, for the rest of this chapter we shall approach the Bible as if it were a kind of drama, something like a Shakespearean play in five acts. The prophetic theme will not seem particularly obvious at first, but as the play progresses we shall find that it emerges quite vividly and gives real coherence to the whole.

Let us proceed to the task. Imagine you are at a theatre. The stage is, of course, the ancient world, but before the curtain rises a narrator appears to explain the context of the play. He reads us the prologue, which is Genesis 1-11.

PROLOGUE: *Paradise Lost (Gen. 1-11)*.

When God made the earth and everything in it, he 'saw that it was good.' That statement is repeated six times in Gen. 1 and at the end of the chapter it is added that 'God saw all that he had made, and it was very good.' We see him put man in charge to rule over it all, and are given a brief, but intimate glimpse of this good earth as he first intended it to be in the Garden of Eden, where we find ourselves in a kind of everyman's paradise, a place of rustic idyll and harmony. God's purpose for the world and for man in it was clearly good, but man chose other ways than God's and because of them lost his paradise (ch. 3). Sin, suffering and death multiplied and soon the narrator is saying, 'God saw how corrupt the earth had become' and 'his heart was filled with pain' (6:12,6). In sending the flood God demonstrated his righteous anger at what man had done to his good earth, but it did not present his final solution, and so sin and its consequences continued to multiply, culminating in Gen. 11 in the Babel fiasco and the consequent division of the languages of earth. The final picture of man's plight is one of complete alienation, of man from man and man from God.

We are thus confronted with the dramatic questions around which our play will revolve: Can God rescue his world? And if so, how? Or will sin continue to thwart his original good purposes?

The Drama of Salvation

The story is therefore to be about the restoring of paradise or Eden. In the garden there were two special trees: the tree of the knowledge of good and evil and the tree of life. Driven from the garden man now has access to neither. He had tasted of one and that left him in a condition of sin, in need of forgiveness. Deprived of the other, his only future is death. These two trees represent the twin poles or foci of our drama, which is to be about God restoring man to a right relationship with both, first through his patriarchs, priests, prophets and kings, then more fully through Jesus and the Church, and finally in his New Heaven at the end of time.

ACT 1: God's Covenant with Abraham—His Call and Promise (Gen. 12-50; c. 200-1300 BC)

The curtain rises with Abraham on stage being called by God to leave his homeland and co-operate with him in his plan to restore his world. We hear God promise him a new home and descendants, indeed that he will be father to a great nation, that he will grant him personal blessing and that ultimately through him all peoples on earth will be blessed (12:1-3). The story that follows tells how Abraham responded to that promise. Today he is remembered as a giant of faith who trusted God and to whom that was reckoned as righteousness (Rom. 4; Heb. 11), but the story itself reveals that that reputation was not won without a number of trials and crises.

We watch him set out in obedience to God's call and almost immediately arrive in the land to which he promised to take him (12:5-7), but then, at the first sign of difficulty, when famine strikes, he goes off to Egypt (12:10). The consequences are disastrous, for he loses his wife to Pharaoh and we see immediately how such a faithless act endangers the promise of God. Not only is he removed from the place where God's purpose is to be worked out, but he also loses the wife through whom his descendants must come. The dramatic question of the prologue is thus vividly highlighted again right at the beginning of the play: Will not man's natural weakness thwart God's will?

However, God intervenes himself and Abraham is ordered out of Egypt. Back in Canaan God reassures him that this is the land where he must stay and which his descendants must possess (13:14-17). Nevertheless, the temptation to return to Egypt remains. Later in his life he sets off in the same direction again, but is stopped before he gets very far, at Gerar, by developments so similar to those in ch. 12 that they again remind and warn us vividly of the consequences of acting contrary to the will of God (ch. 20).

The rest of the Abraham stories are of a similar nature. Several times God reasserts his promises of land, offspring and blessing, but Abraham and his wife find waiting for their fulfilment difficult. There are some momentous occasions when Abraham demonstrates either a simplicity or a heroism of faith that enables him to rise above any doubts or weaknesses, as when God affirmed his covenant with him in ch. 15, or when God demanded the sacrifice of Isaac in ch. 22. But on the whole we find ourselves caught up in a story full of dramatic tension in which we watch God repeatedly rescuing and sustaining in his own divine purposes a very human Abraham.

The Isaac stories only serve to remind us that that tension continues through each successive generation. Abraham had to learn his lessons about abiding in God's will through suffering the consequences of his failure to do so. Isaac too was tempted to go to Egypt in time of famine. The story in Gen. 26 of his visit to Gerar is almost an exact replay of the accounts of Abraham's visit there and his earlier visit to Egypt. Abraham's Egyptian fiasco was rounded off with God's voice urging him to remain in Canaan; Isaac's visit to Gerar is prefaced with a similarly emphatic command to the same effect. The lesson is manifest.

The Jacob stories introduce even greater dramatic crises. To begin with, Jacob himself is presented as a most unlikely person to be the bearer of the covenant, one who cheats his father and his brother, a coward who runs away, a spoiled, mother's child. The early stories of his flight, his marriages, his life on his uncle's farm, and his return home are mostly concerned to show us how he grew in grace and matured in faith. Eventually he emerges as a figure of some stature, but only after we have been kept in some considerable suspense, again asking the same questions as before about human frailty endangering God's purposes.

The next generation brings a different set of problems with it. We now have twelve sons as bearers of the promise, the nucleus of Israel, and our attention focuses more on family relationships. Again there is a spoiled child, Joseph, and his brothers hardly live in love and harmony with each other. Certainly we have a land and descendants now, but it looks as if these family tensions must cause the purpose of God to disintegrate before our very eyes? However, his guiding hand continues to operate and Joseph is whisked off to Egypt, out of reach of his murderous brothers. There he learns maturity, but as the story progresses we see the other brothers follow him into exile in time of famine. It is becoming an all too familiar story. The lesson Abraham had to learn, and Isaac too, has apparently been forgotten and the curtain falls on a family settled outside the land of God's appointing.

All now may seem lost—but not entirely. We note that old Jacob, for one, had not forgotten the lessons Abraham and Isaac had learned (46:1-4). And right at the end of this act, at this critical point in history, the last words we hear are in the dying speech of Joseph, reminding his brothers of the promise of God, that he will one day take them home to Canaan, the place where his purpose must be worked out (50:24). Nonetheless, we cannot but ask how God can possibly redeem this situation now. And even more, how can he ever restore paradise through people such as these, people who are indeed very like you and me?

ACT 2: God's Covenant with Moses—His Word is Revealed (Exodus - 1 Samuel; c. 1300-1000 BC)

Thus far our play has the makings of a classic tragedy, the various characters weaving for themselves a web of catastrophe in the face of potentially great happiness. The curtain rises this time on a people lost in slavery in a foreign land, with no hope but a faint memory of some promise that had been made to their ancestors, crying to God from their bondage and groaning under their intolerable burdens.

The story of Moses' call introduces a ray of hope, but the odds against him seem impossible. However, his dogged adherence to God's promise of complete release for Israel begins to look like the sort of faith we know is needed. Exod. 1-15, though full of dramatic tension, is a story of triumph, illustrating how total and unflinching faith in God permits the ready fulfilment of his purpose. The exodus from Egypt was not without pain, but it was successful.

Israel is again free to pursue the will of God. But a new phase in history calls for a new expression of his purpose in it. God made a covenant with Abraham which has now attained partial fulfilment. That covenant remains and will ultimately require complete fulfilment, but for now God introduces another, a new blue-print for his people's lives and hopes, the covenant at Mount Sinai. At its heart are the Ten Commandments (Exod. 20), but its theme is basically: Hold fast to God, keep his laws, and you will prosper; fail to do that and you will correspondingly fail to prosper. (cp. Deut. 11:26ff; 30:15ff)

The wilderness generation let go of faith and rebelled and so was not permitted to enter the promised land (Num. 14:26-35; Ps. 95:8- 11). However, their descendants under Joshua proved obedient and successfully occupied Canaan (Joshua). But succeeding generations failed to walk in their ways. At the climax of the settlement Joshua and the people reaffirmed the covenant with Moses (Josh. 23-24), but the book of Judges is a tale of repeated rebellion and apostasy with attendant consequences in suffering and oppression. It is the faith of a few individuals and the action of the Spirit alone that preserve the people from total extinction, and by the end of Act Two we see the accumulated effects of continued sin. Central Palestine is occupied by the Philistines and God's chosen people are once more enslaved, those through whom we had hoped he was going to bring blessing to all the families of the earth. Like Act One, Act Two offers us little hope for fulfilment of that promise in the end. Certainly we are back in Canaan, but the situation is hardly more encouraging than it had been at the end of Joseph's life. We seem to be no nearer to the Garden of Eden than we ever were. To be sure, we now have a nation and it is in its promised land, but the final picture of them hardly inspires great hope that they will ever be a source of blessing to all peoples on earth. They are scarcely a blessing to themselves, let alone others. Sin still has far too strong a hold on them.

However, in the last moments before the curtain goes down we again see glimmerings of hope, as God's Spirit raises the young Samuel up to be a revivalist prophet (1 Sam. 1-3, 7), others to be prophets with him (1 Sam. 10, 19), and finally a king, Saul, who was himself endued with the same prophetic Spirit (1 Sam. 9-11). Clearly God has not abandoned his people or his purpose. There is still hope for better things.

ACT 3: God's Covenant with David—His Spirit is revealed (1 Samuel - 2 Kings; c. 1000-540 BC)

Abraham had been called to begin the execution of God's purpose in the first phase of redemption history, Moses in the second, and now it is David in the third. After an unhappy attempt by the beleaguered nation to obtain its freedom through the establishment of a monarchic system under Saul, the throne goes to David, with whom God makes a third covenant. It neither supersedes nor annuls the earlier two, but supplements them with a promise of a royal dynasty through which God intends eventually to bring his will to fulfilment (2 Sam. 7).

As this act unfolds, we have a most encouraging glimpse of initial success. David is able, not only to throw off the Philistine yoke, but also to establish an empire for Israel. The prosperity and security he bequeaths to his son, Solomon, enables the historian to write: 'The people of Judah and Israel were as numerous as the sand on the seashore; they ate, they drank and they were happy.' (1 Kings 4:20) The idyll of Eden has been recaptured—though not for long. Towards the end of his reign, we discover, Solomon turned to other gods (ch. 11), with the disastrous consequence that on his death his kingdom split in two, never to be reunited.

The history of both kingdoms that follows is one of gradual dissolution. Monarch after monarch, with only a few exceptions, is said to have 'committed all the sins his father had done before him', until the Northern Kingdom is wiped off the map by the Assyrians in 722 BC and Jerusalem is taken by the Babylonians in 597 and destroyed ten years later. Both the Assyrians and the Babylonians deported large numbers of the population of Israel and Judah to various parts of their empires, and so the curtain falls at the end of Act Three on a people once more removed from the land of God's promise and once more lost in slavery and oppression. The pattern is becoming all too familiar, as also is the dramatic question it continues to raise: Is God's will to go on being thwarted by man's infidelity like this—possibly for ever?

Happily there were those in Israel who were convinced that the answer to that question must be a resounding 'No'. Beginning in Act Two and continuing through Act Three we see on our stage the birth and growth of a movement for revival led by those we call prophets. They were Israel's charismatics, the religious enthusiasts on whom God's Spirit rested. Their movement first appears in Samuel's time, in the eleventh and tenth centuries, when it is primarily a movement for revival in the face of enervating decadence. It resurfaces with vigour in the ninth century under the leadership of Elijah and Elisha, this time engaged in a life and death struggle for renewal of faith through the power of the Spirit against the baals of Canaanite paganism. From the eighth century on they adopt yet another guise, still charismatic, but now featuring more as preachers and teachers, as spokesmen of God's word, calling men back to the ancient standards of righteousness and justice (Amos), to knowledge of God and responsiveness to his love (Hosea), to repentance, holiness and faith (Isaiah). In the seventh century the same message is reiterated by men like Zephaniah and Jeremiah, and in the sixth by Ezekiel and Isa. 40-55.[12]

The main burden of these later prophets is to highlight the terrible dangers of faithlessness. We hear them constantly warning of coming renewed suffering, destruction and exile. But running through this rather heavy preaching is a thread of hope. There is little more than a glimmering of it in Amos, but starting with him and continuing through the others, particularly Hosea, Isaiah, Jeremiah and Ezekiel, we trace a growing vision that tells of a further act to our play. It speaks of the Lord's people restored to their homeland and of yet another covenant being made with them. This time, however, there is to be a difference, for the prophets tell that in the coming age the new covenant 'will not be like the covenant I made with their fathers . . . because they broke my covenant' (Jer. 31:32). The difference will be firstly that God will give his people a completely new start by wiping their slate clean: 'For I will forgive their wickedness and will remember their sins no more' (31:34), and secondly that he will write this new covenant in their hearts in such a way that they will all 'know the LORD' (31:33f). That is, he will take away their sin and give them an inner will to be faithful.

Ezekiel also speaks of this double aspect of the new covenant hope, but introduces the Spirit as the means whereby God will make it effective: 'I will put my Spirit in you and move you to follow my decrees and be careful to keep my laws' (Ezek. 36:27). The implication is that in the coming new covenant age the prophetic Spirit, with which the prophets themselves are endowed, will become the common possession of all, that is, that all will become charismatics—and furthermore that that is to be the way in which God intends to secure man's full and proper

---

[12] The Book of Isaiah is arranged in three main parts relating to different periods in Israel's history: chs. 1-39 to the eighth century, 40-55 to the latter part of the exile in the mid-sixth, and 56-66 to the restored community at the end of the sixth.

response to his will for the fulfilment of his purposes. This impression is reaffirmed in Isa. 44:3:

> *For I will pour water on the thirsty land,*
> *and streams on the dry ground;*
> *I will pour out my Spirit on your offspring,*
> *and my blessing on your descendants.*

And finally, in the teaching of Joel cited at the head of this chapter we find its clearest expression, the most emphatic prophecy of a general outpouring of the Spirit to endue men with prophetic gifts and abilities.

The expectation itself was actually much more primitive. Moses once expressed the hope, 'I wish that all the LORD'S people were prophets and that the LORD would put his Spirit on them!' (Num. 11:29) That was said on an occasion when the Spirit fell on seventy of his elders in a visitation of God a bit like an Old Testament foretaste of Pentecost.

What is recognised in all these passages is that charismatic or prophetic endowment makes men enthusiasts for God, with a more vivid awareness of God than is ordinary to men, even religious men, and a keener desire to do his will, indeed more than that, with a spiritual gifting and empowering to perform it.

While the prophets focus our hope on the raising up of a race of prophetical men, they also teach that the work of raising them up, or the final act of our play, is to be inaugurated, like each earlier act, by one individual who will himself be the first charismatic of the new age, one on whom the Spirit of the Lord is to rest (Isa. 11:2). To ensure continuity with the covenants of the past, this man is to be a descendant of David (11:1), through his action the righteous relationships required in the covenant with Moses are to be established (11:3-5), and the wider promise of universal blessing made to Abraham is to come to fulfilment as a consequence of his ministry, and so ultimately the peace of Eden itself is to be regained (11:6-9).

Hence we see that much was expected for this coming age, nothing short of the radical fulfilment of all God's promises and the complete restoration of his initial purposes in creation. However, the way the play has unfolded so far seems more to suggest that history has proved such a vision impossible, little more than enthusiastic froth and bubble with no really worthwhile substance for lasting hope.

ACT 4: The Close of the Old Covenant Age—a Time of Waiting (Ezra, Nehemiah, etc.; 540 BC - BC/AD)

In 539 BC a restoration took place. Babylon fell to the Persians and the exiles were permitted to return home. Many Jews did return and they re-established a community in and around Jerusalem under their leaders, Joshua and Zerubbabel, encouraged by the prophets Haggai and Zechariah, and then about a century later under Ezra and Nehemiah.

The early aspirations of those who returned were not quickly realised and in the late fifth century the voice of prophecy fell silent (Joel and Malachi), but not before it had painted some of our most encouraging pictures of hope for the future for God's people (see especially Isa. 56-66[13]). Judaism then became generally more ritualistic and legalistic. Parties such as those later represented by the Pharisees, Sadducees, Essenes and Zealots began to emerge and rather than a picture of coherence and blessing, we find only increasing tension and squabbling. Early in the second century a glimmer of optimism was engendered by the independence gained for Israel under the Maccabean kings[14], but by the end of the first century BC the land was well and truly in subjection once more, this time to the Romans.

We must surely be tempted now to feel that the great purposes of God and the exciting hopes of the prophets have finally fizzled out in

---

[13] See note 12 above.
[14] The story is told in the Apocryphal books, 1 & 2 Maccabees.

complete stagnation. And yet there was still an Israel, and still its religion retained those hopes at its centre.

ACT 5: The New Covenant—The Dawn of the Age of the Spirit (The New Testament; BC/AD - the end of time)

Every good play ends with a denouement in the final act, and ours is no exception. We see the birth of Messiah accompanied by a sudden resurgence of prophetic activity. The angel Gabriel tells Zechariah that his son, John the Baptist, 'will be filled with the Holy Spirit . . . And he will go on before the Lord, in the spirit and power of Elijah' (Luke 1:15,17), and after the boy's birth, Zechariah himself 'was filled with the Holy Spirit and prophesied' (1:67). His wife, Elizabeth, also speaks in the power of the Holy Spirit when she hears of Jesus' conception (1:41f). Then when the baby Jesus is taken to the Temple, he is received by Simeon, who is 'moved by the Spirit', and old Anna, who is called 'a prophetess' (2:25-7,36).

After 400 years of silence the prophetic Spirit is clearly stirring on the earth once more. Having followed the play as we have, our hopes must surely begin to rise again. Are not these the first stirrings of the dawning of the age of the Spirit we have been waiting for?

Jesus, like the boy Samuel in his early years, simply grows up, increasing in wisdom and maturity, until he is about thirty, when the Holy Spirit descends on him and he begins his own charismatic, prophetic ministry. The simplest account of it is the one he himself gave to the messengers from John the Baptist in terms of the prophecy of Isa. 61:1-4 about Spirit-filled ministry, that 'The blind receive sight, the lame walk, those who have leprosy are cured, the deaf hear, the dead are raised, and the good news is preached to the poor.' (Luke 7:22) As we watch the crowds flock to hear him and to feel his healing touch, we begin to experience a renewal of hope in the ancient promises of God, for we are watching before our very eyes the unfolding of that pattern the prophets had foretold. So now we expect to see some hint that Jesus' ministry is going to lead to the creation of the long awaited prophetic community. We are therefore further encouraged as we watch him choose his disciples and particularly when we hear him prepare them for receiving the Holy Spirit themselves (cp. Luke 11; John 14-16). Perhaps we find ourselves disappointed by their failure to understand Jesus' teaching about this and other aspects of what is happening, but we must be even more distressed by the rejection Jesus himself experiences, particularly in religious circles. And so we realise that the old question, whether God's will can ever succeed in the face of such human blindness, is still an urgent one. Our consternation increases as we read of Jesus' betrayal, his desertion by his followers, and finally of his death. For a moment it seems the drama has ended and that all its charismatic enthusiasm has amounted to nothing, but then we read of the resurrection, the regathering of the disciples and their last instruction about waiting for the Spirit, and we realise that we are still only at the beginning of this final act in history.

In the Acts of the Apostles we learn how the Spirit came, how Peter, by citing Joel's prophecy, identified his coming with the birth of the prophetic community, and how in the weeks and years that followed that community established itself in the prophetic life the Spirit gave it. The sick continued to be healed, the apostles saw visions, they spoke with angels, they prophesied, they created communities of love, joy and peace, they showed themselves to be men and women who, as Jeremiah had foreseen, were cleansed and forgiven and who had the will of God implanted in their hearts. The fire of their enthusiasm was contagious and soon the charismatic ministries of men like Peter, Philip and Barnabas were spreading the good news up and down the Palestinian coastlands. After Paul joined them, the gospel spread rapidly through Asia and into Greece, still establishing itself amid 'demonstration of the Spirit's power' (1 Cor. 2:4). Christians with pentecostal gifts were now to be found all over the ancient world: in Rome (Rom. 12:6), Corinth (1 Cor. 12-14), Galatia (Gal. 5:16-26), Ephesus (Acts 19:1-7; Ephes. 4),

Colosse (Col. 1:9), Thessalonica (1 Thes. 5:19-21), as well as in Judea and Samaria (Acts 2 & 8).

Of course there were still tensions, problems, squabbles and the like. The New Testament does not camouflage that fact. For example, in Acts 15 we see something of Paul's quarrel with the Jewish Christians in Jerusalem, and at the end of that chapter we discover he had a rather sharp disagreement with Barnabas and Mark. But the essential message of the New Testament story is that the age of the Spirit has come, first in Jesus and then in his disciples, who prove themselves to be men like the Old Testament prophets, men such as the Old Testament believed God would raise up to fulfil his purpose in bringing blessing to all the families of the earth. Eden is not exactly restored, but there is an Eden-like quality about life in the early Christian community, where joy is one of the chief characteristics of its members. Since the world as a whole still remains under God's curse and in need of redemption, our drama continues to be played out with many of the same tensions and uncertainties as before, but there is now a new factor in it, for the followers of Christ have been granted access again to the source of life, lost since Eden, from which they can draw strength for the role they must play in the continuing outworking of God's purpose. Sin with respect to the tree of the knowledge of good and evil is now atoned for by the sacrifice of Christ, 'the Lamb of God, who takes away the sin of the world', and the wholesome virtue of the tree of life is now embodied in the gift of Christ, 'who will baptise with the Holy Spirit' (John 1:29,33). In the power of the grace and Spirit he supplies, his followers now live the Eden-life in considerable measure, as Ezekiel and other prophets had said they would. And that is very much a charismatic or prophetic quality of life.

In a sense Act Five has no proper ending. In it we see the beginning of a movement that offers a better defined and more assured hope than was found in old Israel, and that hope rests entirely in the freer action of the Spirit in this world through the charismatic followers of Jesus. It was his

The Drama of Salvation

ministry that released that power, and as it takes its origin in him, so also it must find its end in him.

EPILOGUE: Paradise Regained (Revelation)

Today almost 2,000 years have passed and the hard truth is that Eden has still not been restored. History is littered with evidence of man's continuing unfaithfulness. And, the record of the Christian Church has not always been that good! So we are compelled in all honesty, even at this stage, to raise once more the question that has dogged us throughout our drama: Can God's purpose ever really be fulfilled?

But again we can approach it with hope. At the end of the first century, John, one of Jesus' original disciples, was granted a vision in which he saw down the course of history to come, through many times of trial, to God's final hour, to the blessings of Eden fully restored and man in Christ reigning at the last as he was intended to do at the beginning. It is towards the hope engendered by this further vision of Eden's final accomplishment in what John calls the New Jerusalem that Act Five tends. That, however, is in itself a further indication of the prophetic quality of New Testament faith, for it is of the very essence of prophecy to have some such future vision. Hence this final act is, and must always be, one led and dominated by the eschatological race of prophets, men who in some measure share in the vision and experience of the ancient prophets, men such as those whom today we would commonly call prophetic. Their vision, like that of the Old Testament prophets, is still an urgent and excited one, still forward looking, and still one of hope for a glorious finale. It is surely significant that as the curtain falls on the New Testament stage we hear John's voice say, 'He who testifies to these things says, "Yes, I am coming soon." Amen. Come, Lord Jesus.' (Rev. 22:20)

In the time that has passed since then the gospel has indeed reached many peoples and the end John saw is now nearer than most care to imagine. The power of God's Word and his Spirit that worked in creation, that has upheld God's purposes through history, that motivated his prophets, that lived in Christ, that gives us a foretaste of Eden today, still works for the final recreation of all things.

CHAPTER NINE

The Charismatic, the Academic Theologian and the Word of God

But you will receive power when the Holy Spirit comes on you; and you will be my witnesses.

(Acts 1:8)

The drama-outline in the last chapter in no way covers every aspect of Old and New Testament teaching and theology. For example, it says little about the sacrificial systems of the Old Testament, or the wisdom literature, or the Psalms, or the role of satan, or the atoning work of Christ, or the holiness of God. All that can be claimed for it is that it is a conspectus of history against which a charismatic's understanding of the Bible makes sense. By occupying more space and lengthening the discussion much of the missing material could be incorporated into our account, for we have already seen earlier that the charismatic would regard most of the biblical material as prophetically sympathetic literature anyhow. But books like Job, or Proverbs, or Psalms are hardly the sort that can easily be woven into a historical drama. They are more in the nature of deposits of insights gained, or of praises sung by the actors on their journey through the play.

A Living Drama in which we are invited to participate

Sometimes the literature, rather than illustrating charismatic experience, depicts the responses of those who have not appreciated it, as in the case of Job's counsellors, for instance. Our Bible is no simple-minded manual containing naive descriptive outlines of what prophetic religion should be like, but rather a dramatic account of the lives, experiences and insights of men and women who themselves came into living experience of that kind of religion or into contact with other living exponents of it. It is essentially the story of the dynamic activity (the Spirit) of God and of men's varied responses to that. Hence it tells not only of prophets, but also of judges and wise men, of kings and warriors, of craftsmen and fishermen, indeed of all sorts and conditions of people. It paints pictures of men who acted by the power of the Spirit, but equally of men who did not; it paints pictures of times when the Spirit was very active in history, but equally of times when religion was decadent or arid. But always the measure or the ideal is that picture of the eschatological Church of the Spirit, that race of prophetical men whose purpose is to see Eden restored. It is to that end that the whole drama moves, and so it finds its apex in the life-story of the one who ushered in the final age of the Spirit, Jesus Christ.

Its contemporary value derives from the observation of the continuity of his work in the apostolic Church and the implication of the whole drama that that work should still be continued today. It bids us align ourselves with Jesus and the apostles, to share their experience, to come out of Acts One to Four, or out of the audience, and join the players in Act Five, to wait in our own Jerusalems until we too are endued with the same power from on high. Then once we do that, we find the curtain (or the veil) removed altogether and ourselves on stage holding hands with the apostles and seeing everything from their pentecostal perspective.

For a biblical scholar acceptance of that invitation creates an immediate problem. The academic task requires that he stand, as it were, off-stage, like a critic or reviewer, so that he can observe the drama with the more objective eye of scholarship, whereas the Holy Spirit draws him on stage to act with the actors. Thus he finds himself pulled in two directions, the one calling him to stand back and analyse what he sees, the other urging him forward to participate in the action. Ideally, I suppose, it ought to be possible to do both, as indeed it should be in ministerial training institutions, but in the critical atmosphere of academic theology the tension is considerable, often even unbearable.

Communicating Spiritual Truths in Scholarly Language

There is another aspect to this dilemma, one that is perhaps best illustrated through a brief biographical comment. I was myself attracted to the life of scholarship in the first instance by what I then called 'the riddle of the Bible'. To me, as indeed to so many others, the meaning of Scripture was by no means as evident as it has now become. While it attracted me as God's Word, the book itself was an enigma. It purported to be a deposit of revelation, but for the most part all that was revealed to me in it was a series of puzzles, albeit exceedingly fascinating ones. And so I spent many hours discussing the problem of Deuteronomy, the problem of Mark's gospel, the problem of Christ, the problem of faith, and so forth. The essential message of Scripture quite simply eluded me, as it did everyone else with whom I discussed these problems, or at least as it seemed to do, since no-one was able to provide me with answers that satisfied. And so, failing to find anyone who could guide me through the maze, I came to regard scholarship as a tool which might somehow unearth the Bible's hidden meaning, but only gradually and after many years of hard study by many hard working, highly educated men. The field was far too vast for any one scholar to handle alone. My own part must therefore be that of making some small contribution to a sum total of international scholarship that might some day produce something like a satisfactory solution to the riddle of the Bible. I must, however, admit to an increasing sense of despondency as the more I pursued this quite limited objective, the more aware I became of the confused complexity of theological debate, and proportionately I despaired of scholarship ever discovering a solution.

It was for reasons almost entirely unrelated to these that I one day asked God to baptise me with his Holy Spirit just as he had done for his early disciples and seemed to be doing for an ever-increasing number of Christians in our time, but subsequent to that, and to my own great surprise, I found myself reading my Bible with completely new understanding. The veil Paul spoke about had been lifted and for the first time in my life I discovered that it all made very good sense. The riddle had quite simply vanished—yes, in a moment of time—and over the days and weeks that followed, as I watched the jigsaw of the various books and chapters of the Bible progressively reforming themselves into a coherent whole, I marvelled that I had not seen it all before.

It was an exhilarating discovery, but also a painful one, for it deprived me of most of my former scholarly purpose. It could no longer be my aim to help resolve the riddle of the Word of God; the Holy Spirit had done that for me. My studies had now manifestly to change focus, off my search for meaning and onto clarification of my new understanding. Similarly, the focus of my teaching had to change, off presenting the current state of scholarly opinion and debate and onto communicating my new discoveries.

Now, this is precisely the point at which the real acuteness of my dilemma becomes manifest. Since my insight into the coherence of Scripture has not come by purely academic processes, it is difficult to communicate it in purely academic terms. In a sense there is an analogy with matrimonial love. A man who loves his wife will understand what I mean when I say that I love my wife, but I find it well nigh impossible to explain the nature of my love to anyone else. The words I use may convey an impression of something good, intimate, happy and worthwhile, but will scarcely satisfy the man who persists in asking for definitions. Similarly, those with spiritual experience comparable with my own will usually understand what I say without me having to explain too much, whereas others will mostly fail to grasp my meaning. In other words, I realise that the Spirit of truth is more capable of leading others into all the truth than I can ever hope to be, even with my accumulated wisdom and learning.

Here is no theoretical difficulty, but a very practical one. I have discovered over the past seventeen years, indeed to my great frustration at times, that baptism in the Spirit can often give less literate people a much better appreciation of the message of the Bible than three years of university education in a theology department can give to more intellectually capable undergraduates, or a similar period of study in a theological college or seminary to ordinands. However, this observation is not really much different from that made by Paul, for example, whose experience in this respect seems to have been remarkably similar to my own, for he was firmly convinced that the truth about Christ and him crucified, or 'God's secret wisdom' could never be communicated as successfully through careful and erudite presentations of the gospel message as through 'demonstration of the Spirit's power' or when 'God has revealed it to us by his Spirit' (1 Cor. 2:1-10). We may likewise recall how even Jesus' teaching was not so easily understood by his own disciples before their experience of the Spirit at Pentecost as after it.

Unfortunately statements of this kind can and do convey an impression of arrogance, particularly to those who are engaged in the work of biblical scholarship, but as we have already noted, that in itself is part of the charismatic's dilemma, also shared with the early apostles, and so I can do little more about it than Paul did when he wrote to the Corinthians, namely apologise for not being able to express myself about it more acceptably and assure the reader that the intention is quite the converse (2 Cor. 10). My own debt to biblical scholarship is very great and can certainly not all be laid aside.

The Spirit makes us Witnesses, not Analysts

A third major area of tension between a charismatic's experience and his scholarship lies in his shared experience with the apostles and the prophets of a compulsion to speak about his new vision. Just before the ascension, according to Acts 1:8, Jesus forewarned his disciples that receiving the Holy Spirit would turn them into witnesses. Now there is a world of difference between the activities of scholarly research and witnessing. The academic will probe and analyse, or debate and hypothesise, until he finds a solution that seems to him reasonable. He may be himself convinced of its rightness, though he will recognise that further research either by himself or by other scholars may cause him to modify his views, and so he will want to present his findings in print for wider, more public discussion and debate. The charismatic cannot adopt such an approach to his disclosures. His conviction of their essential rightness is based on revelatory experience, the confirmation of the Word, and his own corresponding faith, not on experimental investigation or argument, and consequently is much more absolute. He feels little desire to proffer them simply for discussion, but feels more like an explorer who has discovered a new world and wants to tell everyone else about it, inviting them to come and see it and even to settle in it with him. Hence charismatic writing is seldom publication of ideas or theories for debate, but witness, the declaring of what has been 'seen and heard' (cp. Matt. 11:4; Acts 2:33; 4:20). Here is no mere dogged determination to do something about Jesus' commission to evangelise, but rather an eagerness to proclaim what the Spirit has revealed. If the charismatic is unhappy about purely academic analysis of his vision, he is equally unhappy about evangelical pressurisation. He does not see his function as one of persuasion, but simply of declaration. He is not trying to convince others of the rightness of a theory, but to tell them of his discovery, like the explorer tells of his new country. There is nothing to debate, even if his hearers are sceptical. He is quite simply a witness.

Now witnessing, the declaring of what one has 'seen and heard', is not an academic exercise. It may claim to be a presentation of truth that has not been seen by other scholars, but in itself it has nothing scholarly about it. It is the audience, or the jury, that finds itself engaged in the academic work of testing the witness, but the witness himself can never change his story if he is to remain true to what he has seen and heard. He simply cannot engage in the academic task at that level any more, for if he does, he admits the possibility that his witness may not be true. And there also lies a dilemma.

Much of what I have written here may seem to add to the impression we touched on at the end of Chapter Four, that there is something anti-intellectual in the prophetic mentality. The impression is an unfortunate one, for his experience usually stimulates the charismatic to very deep thought about God, the Bible, and the needs of his society. It is not that he ceases to think theologically, but quite the contrary. However, his theological perspective has changed, indeed so radically that he finds his views no longer fit with those of so many of today's biblical theologians, and furthermore that he fails to find much satisfaction from participating in their debates. It is my convinced opinion that a charismatic's view of the Bible must be different from everyone else's, be they fundamentalists, conservatives, liberals, radicals, or whatever. Their views are based on doctrines, assumptions and hypotheses, sometimes diametrically opposed ones, about the nature of Scripture and revelation. The charismatic's is based on what he finds himself thinking after he is baptised in the Holy Spirit. And as we have seen, his discovery is itself more in the realm of experience than doctrine, for it is a discovery that he has stepped out of the audience into the play where he shares in so many, if not ultimately all, of the experiences of the actors, particularly of the charismatics/pentecostals of the last act in the New Testament Church.

The Wealth of the Witness of the Spirit

It is for these reasons that this book contains no weighing of the viewpoints of other scholars and no listing of the works of others with whom I am in agreement or disagreement. In one sense there is no debate. Prophetic experience leads me to treasure the biblical records with a new love that makes me less willing to dismiss as much as the liberals tend to do, but it does not persuade me therefore to accept all the historical conclusions of fundamentalism. But then, it tells me of things about which neither of these speak, and there lies its great attraction. The word that comes most readily to mind for describing these things is not fundamentalism, or radicalism, or any other '-ism', but truth. The witness of the Spirit, as Jesus says in John's Gospel, is essentially to truth—not to any truth about technical, historical, or scientific data and statistics, which are properly subjects for scholarly research, but to the truth about the word of God, and that speaks to me of salvation, forgiveness, blessing, hope, love, joy, peace, power and the like. Preeminently that truth is about Jesus, who, as we have it in John's Gospel again, is himself the Truth (14:6). So the Spirit shows me the truth of Scripture (or resolves the riddle of the Bible) and the truth of Jesus (or resolves the riddle of the incarnation), but perhaps the two are one, for even the Bible itself recognises an interplay between the written word and the incarnate Word of God. Both speak of the same truth, and the Spirit witnesses equally to both. That is not to say there is no truth in the things that liberals or conservatives say, but that there is a more profound truth that neither of these, in the charismatic's eyes at any rate, have ever grasped. That alone comes from the Spirit of God, not by any human intellectual process.

Of course, charismatic experience offers no magical solution to so many of the problems that the scholars handle, such as the date of the Exodus, or the editorial arrangement of the book of Ezekiel, or the authorship of the Pastoral Epistles, but it does bear witness to the basic truth of the accounts of what the biblical personalities experienced in their relationships and encounters with God or his messengers, and to the essential truth of their aspirations and hopes for those who believe in Christ. The charismatic's main argument with biblical scholars is therefore about the nature of belief. He wants them to begin believing that what they are reading is not just myth, or legend, or the theological ruminations of pious intellects, if they are liberals, nor simply ancient history or doctrinal presentations, if they are conservatives, but living Christian experience as it was and as it still should be. Like Peter, he wants the critic to lay aside his pen for a moment and to step on stage to see for himself what this Spirit-life is really like. But then any scholar or student who accepts that challenge will find himself, as I do, longing for some new kind of scholarship through which he can express his new-found revelations and understandings.

That, in the end, is the invitation of Scripture itself. Does not our Drama of Salvation end with such a call from the Spirit and the Bride (of Christ; = the Church) who say 'Come!' It is those who are 'thirsty' who will come, and when they do, they will drink of the water of life freely given by God. And that water is the Spirit of God himself, flowing from his throne and the Lamb. Our calling is not so much to receive understanding as to receive life. But in the light of that life there is indeed a freshness of understanding unknown to and unknowable by the natural intellect. The Christian, who has tasted such things and knows that nothing else can satisfy in the same way, must inevitably become a witness—but not without understanding. And that is why the Spirit cuts through all our debates and scholarship to lead us into all truth, his truth.

CHAPTER TEN

That You May Have Life

These are written that you may believe that Jesus is the Christ, the Son of God, and that by believing you may have life in his name.
(John 20:31)

Authentic teaching can never be a mere academic exercise. It is the attempt to interpret the message of salvation to a concrete community in terms that will lead it to repentance and to a deeper openness to the Spirit. When, therefore, Christian teaching loses its prophetic character, it becomes shot through with inauthenticity. It degenerates into cerebral academic exercises.

Donald Gelpi, Charism and Sacrament, p. 88

A book that informs without inspiring may be indispensable to the scientist, the lawyer, and the physician; but mere information is not enough for the minister. If knowledge about things constituted learning, the encyclopaedia would be all the library one needed for a fruitful ministry. The successful Christian must know God, himself, and his fellow men. Such knowledge is not gained by assembling data but by sympathetic contact, by intuition, meditation, silence, inspiration, prayer, and communion. The book that leads the soul out into the sunlight, points upward and bows out is always the best book.

The man who can teach us to teach ourselves will help us more in the long run than the man who spoon-feeds us and makes us dependent upon him. The teacher's best service is to make himself unnecessary. The book that serves as a ramp from which our minds can take off is the best book for us; the book that frees us to think our own inspired thoughts is our friend.

David J. Fant, A. W. Tozer, a twentieth century prophet, 1964, p. 128.

Our purposes in teaching the Word of God should still be the same today as were Jesus' purposes. He came that we might have life in all its fullness (John 10:10) and the gospels were written to help us find that life for ourselves and obtain it. Too much of our theological writing and teaching misses this life-giving dimension completely, and some of it even achieves the converse, destroying the very faith that should bring life—through critical, rational and other totally negative approaches to studying the Scriptures. The need for a new approach is indeed very urgent.

As we have noted Classical Pentecostalism never developed a total Biblical theology of its own, but tended to adopt already existing evangelical and fundamentalist systems of interpretation. Charismatics have mostly done the same, with differing degrees of dissatisfaction since these theological systems, as well as the more liberal ones, generally fail to meet their need to learn more about the ways of the Spirit, the power of faith, revival, healing ministry, the dynamic of the word, etc.—in fact everything that relates to personal experience of God in the life of the believer. What we need, therefore, is an approach that lays bare the life-giving heart of Scripture, one that taps its dynamic source—which is, of course, the Spirit of God himself.

Israel's history, unlike secular history, is mainly a story about God's dealings with men. Its stories of individual lives also focus on the working of God's Spirit in transforming men. And in the telling the Bible delights in the very things many Christians love to hear about today: the miraculous, the prophetic, the visionary, the love and fellowship of Spirit-filled believers, and so forth—the very things that give life. Such matters must become the main focus of our theological studies too, if they are to cease being sterile and become life-giving.

The main purpose of Biblical theology is to give a reasoned account of Christian faith, vision and experience as it is, or should be, grounded in Scripture. Linguistic, historical and topical studies, such as archaeology, textual and literary criticism, Jewish culture and customs, and the like, all contribute to our fuller understanding, but we must never lose sight of that more fundamental purpose, to enable better understanding of the life-giving nature of Biblical faith. In writing The Way of the Spirit I divided my survey into four parts, which taken together give a fairly comprehensive overview of the faith/life dynamic of Scripture. I saw it to be the purpose of the Spirit- filled theologian:

- Firstly, to teach the living dynamic of the basic principles on which all Christian life and experience ought to be founded: faith in God's promises, obedience to his call and acknowledgement of the saving power of Christ's sacrifice.

- Secondly, to explain the main revival thrusts in Biblical history, highlighting the principles by which God's kingdom operates and out lining the challenges and vision that inspire all men of the Spirit.

- Thirdly, to demonstrate how the experiences and teachings, along with the faith and vision, of prophets and other men of the Spirit in both Testaments are of the very essence of Biblical hope.

- Fourthly, to show the life-givingness of the approaches that Spirit-filled Christians and the Bible have in common to worship, service, pastoral matters, the challenges of daily living, and the like.

To tap the life source of the Bible, reading and studying it must be done in conjunction with prayer, and specifically prayer that the Holy Spirit, whose work is to lead into all the truth, will take us behind all that is written by commentators and theologians to show us his truth for ourselves—indeed more than that, that he will lead us to the very source of this truth in the life of God himself. It is important always to remember Jesus' warning: 'You diligently study the Scriptures because you think that by them you possess eternal life. These are the Scriptures that testify about me, yet you refuse to come to me to have life.' (John 5:39f)

As we read our Bibles we must allow ourselves to walk on the stage of the ancient world, first with the men of the Old Testament, and then with Jesus and his disciples—to go with Jesus around Galilee, listen to him speaking, participate in the astonishment and excitement of the crowd, share in the puzzlement and the illumination of his disciples, and so get the feel of what we read, particularly as it relates to the vision, the power and the life of God these men of olden times knew.

Spirit-filled Bible teaching should enable us to read our Bibles in something like the way we watch a play. It should lift us into the life of the drama and enable the power of that life to flow through our lives as we walk and talk with the ancient men of God and above all with Jesus himself. It should help us to lay hold of their vision so that it becomes our vision as well, to grasp their longings so that they become our longings, and similarly their joys that they become our joys, for therein lies the life God wants us to know in Christ.

The Bible can be read for information about the things of God, but also for enjoyment of its life. The first is theology, which on its own too easily becomes the letter that kills, and so it needs to be coupled with the second, if our theology is to be living and life-giving. But that is just how the Scriptures were intended to be read in the first place, for, as the letter to the Hebrews puts it, 'the word of God is living and active . . . it penetrates even to dividing soul and spirit . . . it judges the thoughts and attitudes of the heart.' (Heb. 4:12) The Bible was never intended to be a mere repository of doctrine or information, but the active, life-giving Word of God himself.

When Paul drew his contrast between the letter that kills and the Spirit that gives life, he was writing, not just about Bible reading or Christian experience, but about effectiveness in ministry (1 Cor. 3:6). The Spirit and the Word were not given simply for enjoyment, but so that through them we may minister life to others. If our teaching does not do that, then how will those we teach ever be able to do it?

Paul contrasts the letter and the Spirit in the same chapter in which he speaks of the revelatory effect of the veil being removed, and with that observation our study comes full cycle. It is, however, essential to remember that it is the Spirit that gives life, and in the end everything we have been considering here comes from him, 'from the Lord, who is the Spirit'. The removal of the veil is something that happens once we are baptised and enlightened with the Holy Spirit, and without that foundational experience much of what I have written will seem meaningless, even foolish, as Paul himself said: 'The man without the Spirit does not accept the things that come from the Spirit of God, for they are foolishness to him, and he cannot understand them, because they are spiritually discerned.' (1 Cor. 2:14)

My prayer must therefore be that before all else, you, the reader, before undertaking any further theological study, before embarking on any further teaching, will come to know for yourself what it is to allow God to baptise you with his Holy Spirit so that you can understand the things that come from his Spirit, and then you will learn how to read and to teach so that you receive and give life, God's life. My prayer is that you may truly know what Paul meant when he wrote these words:

You are a letter from Christ . . . written not with ink but with the Spirit of the living God, not on tablets of stone but on tablets of human hearts. . . our competence comes from God. He has made us competent as ministers of a new covenant—not of the letter but of the Spirit; for the letter kills, but the Spirit gives life. . . . Will not the ministry of the Spirit be even more glorious?

. . . their minds were made dull, for to this day the same veil remains when the old covenant is read. It has not been removed, because only in Christ is it taken away. Even to this day when Moses is read, a veil covers their hearts. But whenever anyone turns to the Lord, the veil is taken away. Now the Lord is the Spirit, and where the Spirit of the Lord is, there is freedom. And we, who with unveiled faces all contemplate the

Lord's glory, are being transformed into his likeness with ever-increasing glory, which comes from the Lord, who is the Spirit.

(2 Cor. 3:3-18)

BIBLE READING COURSE

The Way of the Spirit

What are the biblical foundations of life in the Spirit?
What is the Bible all about?

These are the main questions addressed in *The Way of the Spirit Bible Reading Course*, written by John McKay and used by students at Kingdom Faith Ministries' training centres in Britain and overseas. It teaches about the livingness of the Bible and the power of the Spirit revealed in its pages, to help Christians understand: what the Bible is all about, what the way of God's Spirit is in it, and how to enter more fully into the richness of life men of Bible-times enjoyed.

It is arranged in four six-month parts. Each part is self-contained and can be taken on its own, with or without assistance by correspondence. It is ideally suited for group study.

The four parts are:

1: The Call and the Cross—on the theme of God's Call to Faith, Obedience and Sacrifice - covering: Old Testament - Genesis to Deuteronomy; New Testament - Mark's Gospel, Romans and Hebrews.

2: Times of Refreshing—on the themes of Revival, Establishing the Kingdom and Church Growth - covering: Old Testament - Joshua to 2 Kings; New Testament - Matthew, Acts, 1 & 2 Corinthians, Galatians, 1 & 2 Thessalonians.

3: Heirs of the Prophets—on the themes of Prophecy, Revival and Spiritual Gifts - covering: Old Testament - the Prophets from Isaiah to Malachi; New Testament - Luke, selections from Acts and Paul's epistles, Revelation.

4: My Lord and My God—on the themes of Wisdom, Worship and the Sovereignty of God - covering: Old Testament - Ruth, 1 Chronicles to Song of Songs, Lamentations, Daniel, Jonah;   New Testament - John, Ephesians to Colossians, 1 Timothy to Philemon, James to Jude

The teaching materials available for each part are:

1. a commentary-style Bible reading guide,
2. a folder of weekly work-sheets,
3. a set of six tapes, each with four 20-minute talks relating to the week's reading.

Also available in the same flow, but not part of the Bible Course:

- Booklets and tapes on aspects of revival, faith, the Bible, etc.,
- Short (4-6 week) Bible Reading Courses,
- Lectures to Students on various Biblical books on tape.
- Local teaching days, local study groups, conferences, and regional or residential college programmes.

All the above resources in some measure represent an outworking of the longings and principles discussed in this present booklet, which simply outlines the spiritual and theological journeyings that have led to their development.

For further details or to order, please write to:
The Way of the Spirit, Roffey Place, Old Crawley Road, Faygate, Horsham, West Sussex RH12 4RU.
Tel: 01293 851543. Fax: 01293 854610.
E-mail: info@thewayofthespirit.com.
Or visit our web site:
http://www.thewayofthespirit.com